EVETTE ROSE

CW00350279

Transform Everyday

Metaphysical Anatomy™
Healing Quotes for Inspiration

EVETTE ROSE

ISBN: 9781086624830

EVETTE ROSE

ACKNOWLEDGEMENTS

Thank you to my students for your inspiration and Viktor Meier
for your support.

With love
Evette Rose

How to use Transform Everyday

The intention with this book is for you to become aware of your patterns and negative limiting thoughts. As awareness of a problem is a problem half solved. Every day as you progress throughout the book you will answer questions related to the topic and quote for the day. This is where the magic and transformation will start to unfold. You will start to rediscover your relationship with yourself and take gentle steps and actions that can greatly improve your quality of thoughts and life. It's time to become aware of what no longer serves your purpose and to reestablish your relationship with yourself and ultimately your environment and how you express your true authentic self.

As you heal you and take daily steps to heal and change.

Make sure you have a notebook to keep track of your thoughts, feelings and progress.

Please go to www.transformingeveryday.com and sign up to the healing page. You will be given access to meditations and exercises to support you throughout your journey. You can complete any meditation or affirmation tracks that you feel drawn to and resonates with most.

Also feel free to join our support forum www.matsupportforum.com

With love,
Evette Rose

EVETTE ROSE

Day 1

A person who has no bounds and who are living their highest expression of freedom is the one who has nothing to hide.

When you are honest with yourself, you have nothing to hide. Not even from yourself.

Note to myself   Date _____

In which area of your life are you underestimating yourself and your talents?

_____

_____

_____

_____

_____

_____

_____

_____

_____

_____

_____

_____

_____

Day 2

You are too weak," said the mind. "You are also vulnerable," said the heart.

"You are here for a reason, keep moving forward, I've got your back," said the soul.

Stop underestimating yourself. Your path is part of a bigger plan! Keep moving forward.

Note to myself   Date _____

In which area of your life are you underestimating yourself and your talents?

_____

_____

_____

_____

_____

_____

_____

_____

_____

_____

_____

Day 3

If you keep your focus on your goals, dreams and are ferociously dedicated then doors will open. People will feel your passion.

Your positivity will inspire people, perhaps even someone that could open up doors for you.

Note to myself   Date _____

My question to you is, what does your heart desire? Let that desire transpire into your world and hold that strong intention. That intention should be so strong that no one can sway you from your path. You have worked hard for what you have achieved, giving up should not be an option!

_____

_____

_____

_____

_____

_____

_____

_____

_____

_____

Day 4

Anxiety, I have decided to break off our relationship. You no longer serve my purpose. Anxiety can be incredibly debilitating. But what if anxiety is not just a negative and annoying condition?

Anxiety could be related to our intuition telling us that something is wrong, or deep down, we can sense that a significant change in our life is coming. It can also be the result of unresolved and suppressed stress in our lives. I see anxiety as a transition period when you are about to go through a big transformation. It's like the unconscious mind knows that change is coming, and the body is resisting it, as it doesn't know what to expect.

Note to myself   Date _____

Give your anxiety a voice, if you did, what would it say?

_____

_____

_____

_____

_____

_____

_____

_____

Day 5

Oneness is our essential nature. With permission, you can make changes inside yourself that supports and encourages change within another person as the possibility of change is brought into their consciousness.

We are powerful beyond measure; we are the ones that underestimate and undermine our abilities. You can be the change for someone who is stuck.

Note to myself   Date _____

How can you support yourself as much as you are supporting others? What easy and simple steps can you start to take today?

_____

_____

_____

_____

_____

_____

_____

_____

_____

_____

_____

Day 6

Limiting beliefs are symptoms of underlying stress and trauma that have not been given a voice for it to be released.

Get ahead of the game and become aware of what your beliefs are. Meditate on it today and find the source of your dominant negative belief that is holding you back from doing something productive today. How did you feel before a current negative belief was activated when you wanted to complete a task or make an important decision?

Note to myself   Date _____

What do you need to belief in yourself in order to know that you can gracefully overcome this mental block?

_____

_____

_____

_____

_____

_____

_____

_____

_____

_____

_____

Day 7

Multiple limiting beliefs can be tied to a singular traumatic event.

Don't focus on just singular beliefs today. Explore where these beliefs originate. Instead of taking a step, you will take a giant leap in changing not just you, but your genetic patterns! The power is in your hands!

Note to myself   Date _____

What is the emotional theme / pattern connected to your limiting beliefs?   When did it start? What emotional resource did you need at the time of a stressful event that could help to restore your confidence in yourself?

_____

_____

_____

_____

_____

_____

_____

_____

_____

_____

_____

_____

Day 8

When you release emotional blocks within you, it releases the surrounding belief structure that stemmed from the emotional block, allowing the body to return to its natural harmonious state.

We as human beings are designed to be peaceful and harmonious. If we were designed to live our lives in a state of stress and tension, then we wouldn't be suffering from so many different medical conditions.

Note to myself   Date _____

What can you implement and change in your life today to bring more grace, ease and peace into? What do you need to give to yourself first?

_____

_____

_____

_____

_____

_____

_____

_____

_____

_____

Day 9

It is your responsibility to decide how you are going to move forward and away from your past. After all, what happened is in the past. You can start by making small changes in your everyday life. Every change is your conscious effort to move forward in life and to take charge of your future.

Only you can take responsibility for your future. If people are not in alignment with your new changes, then perhaps significant changes are necessary. When you are dedicated to making changes in your life without fighting for it, then the universe will respond. If you fight for change, your need for change will be met with more challenges to fight.

Note to myself   Date _____

What steps can you take today to be kinder to yourself?

_____

_____

_____

_____

_____

_____

_____

_____

Day 10

Know the difference between a fear and a valid instinctive reaction. Knowing the difference between instinctive responses and emotional responses based on past trauma and stress allows you to have the best judgment, especially when you need to make a quick judgment call or an important decision.

I invite you today to become aware of how you make decisions in your life. Are your responses based on past negative experiences that could ultimately cause you to make an error in judgment?

Note to myself   Date _____

When you have to make an important decision and you feel resistance. Feel where you feel the resistance. Give it a voice. What does it say?

_____

_____

_____

Whose voice do you hear that you know, or face do you see that you know? Does this fear belong to you or not?

_____

_____

_____

_____

Day 11

People are like tides and waves of the ocean. Some are gentle, and some are destructive however, they never stay on the beach. They always move away, change, and never come back in the same shape, way, or form.

I have come to learn that people in my life are the same. You can't control tides and waves, and you can't control people. Allow people to come and go in your life without needing to control how they show up or leave. Everything and everyone has a purpose, how long that purpose serves you depends on the experience that you are having. When you grow, change, and heal, these changes will reflect in your life. Be at peace with it. There is a greater plan for you.

Note to myself   Date _____

Which person or situation do you need to let go of or take a break from today in order for you to grow emotionally and spiritually?

_____

_____

_____

_____

_____

_____

_____

Day 12

Openness and receptivity enhance the process of transformation and allows for the most considerable amount of flexibility and impact on one's life. Healing and change have never started by being rigid, holding onto tension, and inflexibility.

Understand though that by being open to changes and new phases doesn't mean you have to be vulnerable. Be open with discernment and healthy loving boundaries.

Note to myself   Date _____

Where in your life can you exercise more loving boundaries and be more flexible?

_____

_____

_____

_____

_____

_____

_____

_____

_____

_____

_____

Day 13

The more clarity you have of your own identity, the more power and impact you will have in terms of awakening that level of clarity within someone else. Get to know yourself, know what your passions are, know your values. Be aware of what you will tolerate or disregard in your life.

Know what your goals are and how you are going to achieve them. This is a recipe for building an unbreakable bond with yourself!

Note to myself   Date _____

What do you feel passionate about today? What can you do differently today to embrace it more and make it your reality?

_____

_____

_____

_____

_____

_____

_____

_____

_____

_____

Day 14

Projection will occur. Remain dissociated, stay in 3rd person yet compassionate. Don't be part of the problem, be part of the solution. Today your mission is to be part of the solution and not the problem.

Even if someone is in the wrong, be patient and observant to see what is really taking place. In most cases you might find that the conflict is not actually the problem, it could perhaps be deep subconscious pain that the other is in.

Note to myself   Date _____

I invite you today to be an observer. Allow others to express themselves. Become aware as to how you can be part of a solution when a challenge arises. Perhaps even if you were faced with a challenge today, what advice would you give yourself in order to improve the situation?

_____

_____

_____

_____

_____

_____

_____

_____

_____

Day 15

Taking personal responsibility means that you were part of a dynamic that caused you pain in one way or another, yet now you are taking control of something that is within your power to control.

That is your future and quality of life. Being happy is an internal state.

You can feel stuck in a room for days, yet you can still feel psychologically free and experience freedom. Freedom is a state of mind, and so is happiness. I invite you today to think about a positive emotional state that you would like to feel. Become aware that this feeling starts from within; it is an emotional state. You cannot rely on your external circumstances to make you happy.

Your circumstances will always change, which means how it affects your emotional state will still be affected. Take your power back and gently learn how to regain control of your emotional state and ultimately, your happiness.

Note to myself   Date _____

From whom do you need to take your power, freedom and happiness back? Visual this person or situation in front of you. You can either out loud or silently in your mind say to this person/s, "I take my power back from you. I take my happiness back from you. I take my freedom back from you." Write down more power affirmations.

_____

_____

_____

Day 16

Patience is not a weakness.

Just because you know when to act and when to be silent doesn't mean that you are weak, it can be perceived as a weakness by someone who takes advantage of another's kindness. Timing is everything

Note to myself   Date _____

What do you need to believe in yourself in order to know that your judgment regarding timing and taking action is in alignment with your needs and circumstances?

_____

_____

_____

_____

_____

_____

_____

_____

_____

_____

_____

_____

Day 17

One unavoidable responsibility that you have in your life is your future and how you choose to live it.

I invite you today to remember that you are in control of your destiny. If you feel that you are not, then perhaps it's time to start making changes. Start small, make small changes and then start making bigger changes. This is a beautiful and gentle way to reconnect with your confidence and self-esteem. Your self-esteem is holding you back. The more confidence you restore within yourself, the bigger the changes will be in your life and ultimately you will experience more freedom.

Note to myself   Date _____

What do you need to believe in yourself in order to know that you no longer have to accept the behavior of a person that challenges your self-esteem?

_____

_____

_____

_____

_____

_____

_____

_____

Day 18

The only thing that stops you from creating what you want in your life is resourceful states of mind and emotion, which is blocked by stressful events from your past. In no way is it worth holding onto the past, there is no benefit.

You only nurture anger and resentment, which robs you of your quality of life. Your life can pass you by as you are not able to take in all the opportunities that are around you. Your energy and focus are zoned in on the past. You inevitably filter out a perfectly happy life that could perhaps be right in front of you.

Note to myself   Date _____

Which part of your past is still alive within you? What do you need to believe in yourself in order to know that you can leave it in the past?

_____

_____

_____

_____

_____

_____

_____

_____

_____

Day 19

You are powerful beyond measure and you have emotional resources available to you. You are an expression of your ancestry.

Your ancestry has experienced every single emotional resource that you could imagine. Your ancestors' experiences and resources are within you!

Note to myself　　　　Date _____

How would you like to emotionally feel at the end of today? Which positive emotional resource would benefit you the most to focus on that could ignite the cellular memory of the desired emotional outcome?

_____

_____

_____

_____

_____

_____

_____

_____

_____

_____

Day 20

Where in your life have you sacrificed your values and the things that were once important to you for the sake of acceptance of another to fit in?

Today is as good as any other day to make a change. Reconnect to your values and what used to be important in life. Redirect your intention and energy back to your values again. Nurture them and re-establish the vision that you had for yourself and your future. Don't be afraid to dream big!

Note to myself   Date _____

Write down at least five values that are important to you i to live your life to the fullest?

Examples: Do things that I love, love myself as much as I love others...

_____

_____

_____

_____

_____

_____

_____

_____

_____

Day 21

When have you abandoned love to achieve superficial goals that took you away from your true authentic self and purpose?

Are you paying the price for lost love, friendship, and a relationship with yourself because you thought that your future and success were in the hands of someone else?

Note to myself   Date _____

To whom have you given the power to be in control of your happiness? What do you need to feel and believe within yourself in order to know that the strong predisposition for happiness is already within you?

_____

_____

_____

_____

_____

_____

_____

_____

_____

_____

_____

Day 22

When did you stop being true to your goals and instead became competitive and stop serving humanity?

There are times when we are so eager to achieve success, to prove that one person is wrong. To prove our self-worth. Failure is not an option. I have to say in most cases this can be a healthy approach, yet there are times when this attitude destroys friendship and love, and you can become isolated.

Note to myself   Date _____

Where in your life have you scarified too much of yourself for the sake of success or to achieve a goal? Where in your life can you create more balance?

_____

_____

_____

_____

_____

_____

_____

_____

_____

_____

_____

Day 23

It's okay to take a break, but never give up! Here is a gentle reminder that you are human; you can only do so much with the energy that you have available to you.

Sometimes we hit a wall or go through a plateau phase. This phase can pass by quickly, yet some of us can become stuck in it. What matters is that you never give up. Start retaking small steps again, burning yourself out will not give you the results that you are trying to achieve

Note to myself   Date _____

When something in your life burns you out, it means that you have either failed to have healthy boundaries with yourself and others, or you are on a path that only drains you and you have lost your passion. Remind yourself what you got you excited about, the very thing that may have caused you to burn out? Meditate and back track your steps to see, feel and sense when you started to lose energy and start to make changes to avoid this mishap in the future.

_____

_____

_____

_____

_____

_____

_____

Day 24

When all your efforts fail, remember that you are the only actor on stage in your life, everyone else is part of the audience. Keep dancing, take the lead, and make it a damn good show.

Failure only means that there is yet another opportunity to explore. It doesn't mean it's the end. It doesn't mean that you are not good enough to do what you love or what you set out to do. Keep moving forward, reassess your approach, your attitude toward your goals.

Note to myself   Date _____

Keep changing the game plan. Make sure that you have positive and passionate people around you and most importantly of all, never stop! Which successful person do you admire? Which aspects of their qualities and mindset can you incorporate into your life?

_____

_____

_____

_____

_____

_____

_____

_____

_____

Day 25

Your self-esteem is a reflection of how you allowed others to treat you in the past.

The fun part about maturing into our adult life is that we start to gain so much more control over our lives. That control includes our self-esteem and how we allow people to affect us emotionally. Ultimately, when someone mistreated you or always criticized, it's their pain that is pouring over, an unconscious outcry for help. You haven't necessarily learned all the tools to communicate your emotions, and neither did they. Emotions can be so complex to put into words, and when they are suppressed you ignore and disconnect from your truth.

Note to myself   Date _____

How can you improve your relationship with yourself today? What kind of negative thoughts do you have toward yourself? Who projected that onto you? What steps can you take today to improve it?

_____

_____

_____

_____

_____

_____

_____

Day 26

If there is passion, then there will be success! Take action now! The message for today is that when you truly believe that you can achieve something, then go for it.

People might not always understand your intentions, goals, and the path that you want to start. Be okay with that. Your soul knows where you are heading toward. If you don't know yourself, be OK with that too. It only means that you need more structure as to what you are planning to do. You need to be clearer in terms of what you need from your environment and how to achieve it in order to make a smoother journey to self-fulfillment and success.

Note to myself   Date _____

How are you holding yourself back from achieving your goals today? What kind of mindset do you need to hold and energize in order to feel confident and ready to take action?

_____

_____

_____

_____

_____

_____

_____

_____

Day 27

Never pity another person. You undermine their ability to cope with their circumstances, some people just need more time to find their way.

Pitying them only leaves a trail of dis-empowerment and unnecessary judgment in their life. Pity is not a form of love, it's often an inaccurate judgment based on very little information. Allow yourself to see the best in another person, especially when they cannot see it themselves.

Note to myself   Date _____

Sometimes it just takes one person's awareness to help another ignite their self-esteem and inner power. What can you change within yourself today in order to ignite someone else's confidence?

_____

_____

_____

_____

_____

_____

_____

_____

_____

Day 28

The art of surrendering is often so misunderstood.

Surrendering is not a sign of weakness; it's when you recognize that what you have been doing and fighting for is no longer of value. Your fear of humiliation and failure is what shapes your values around surrendering.

Surrendering means you have reached a level of awareness and willingness to be open to new options and possibilities that could potentially alter your circumstances. This will open new doorways, which will give you a second chance to make different decisions.

Note to myself　　　Date _____

Have you ever felt like surrendering? Here is a powerful perspective on this subject and I invite you to see it from a different angle today. When in your life did you surrender? Did you really surrender, or did you realize perhaps that a better solution or outcome is possible?

_____

_____

_____

_____

_____

_____

_____

_____

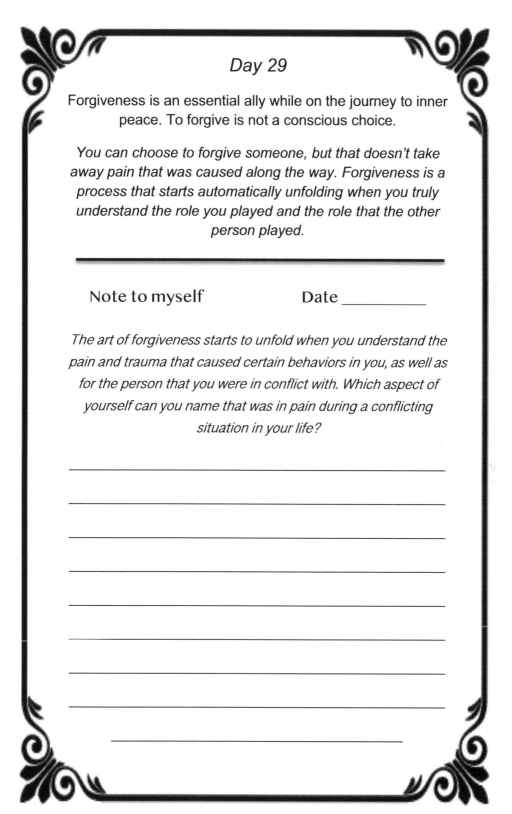

Day 29

Forgiveness is an essential ally while on the journey to inner peace. To forgive is not a conscious choice.

You can choose to forgive someone, but that doesn't take away pain that was caused along the way. Forgiveness is a process that starts automatically unfolding when you truly understand the role you played and the role that the other person played.

Note to myself   Date _____

The art of forgiveness starts to unfold when you understand the pain and trauma that caused certain behaviors in you, as well as for the person that you were in conflict with. Which aspect of yourself can you name that was in pain during a conflicting situation in your life?

_____

_____

_____

_____

_____

_____

_____

_____

_____

Day 30

Burn the foundation of fear. Everything that falls apart after that is only illusions.

Fear is an illusion, yet it can feel so real that it can stop people dead in their tracks.

No one is immune to the games that your mind often plays with you. Understanding why the fear is there in the first place can ultimately set you free.

Note to myself   Date _____

Accepting that fear is there and you can't do anything about it often serves as an excuse, an excuse that becomes an unconscious pattern in your life that stops you from stepping into greatness. Your fear is showing you that are about to step out of your comfort zone. What is your next step going to be today in order to overcome a fear you have?

_____

_____

_____

_____

_____

_____

_____

_____

Day 31

There are times when a situation is not the problem; it is how you respond to it that could contribute to the problem.

Be mindful today of situations where you perhaps could overact.

Become aware of the underlying emotions which may have had nothing to do with the issue that you overacted to. These underlying emotions may have been building up as a result of something in your life that you have been avoiding.

Note to myself   Date _____

Give yourself the gift of freedom and set yourself free from those emotional burdens that only hinder you and negatively affect your judgment. Before you react today, take note of how you feel and then how you felt before the initial (final emotional outcome), is what you feel really relevant to the situation at hand?

_____

_____

_____

_____

_____

_____

_____

_____

Day 32

I don't make mistakes. It's called experimenting!

If you happen to find yourself in a dilemma or made a mistake today, then here is a fun excuse.

Note to myself   Date _____

Where in your life can you be more playful?

_____

_____

_____

_____

_____

_____

_____

_____

_____

_____

_____

_____

_____

_____

Day 33

A little bit of craziness combined with creativity is not necessarily a bad thing! Look at Einstein, brilliant yet living on the edge in so many ways. You also never meet a successful person who is sane.

You don't get to see the crazy side of them. You need a little bit of craziness to be fearless and bold!

Never stop having fun, even when you are creative! Being too serious and rigid will dim your creative light and passion!

Note to myself   Date _____

Your 'homeplay' for today is to keep laughing and keep your attitude positive. What do you need to eliminate in your life in order to be more playful?

_____

_____

_____

_____

_____

_____

_____

_____

_____

_____

Day 34

People complain, "I always have this problem." What they don't realize is that 'always' has a beginning.

We all complain we all have bad days, that's okay! We are human; we can't always be the best versions of ourselves. If you find yourself complaining a lot lately, then I invite you to explore, "When did this ongoing problem that I am complaining about start?"

Note to myself   Date _____

When you feel like complaining today, think of the opposite factor of the complaint instead. Write down your 5 main complaints and then write down the opposite flip side of the complaint.

_____

_____

_____

_____

_____

_____

_____

_____

_____

_____

Day 35

Always show kindness; you never know what is going on in another person's life. *Kindness is free, it doesn't cost you money, time, or energy. We all have hardships. Show kindness today.*

Note to myself   Date _____

Apart from showing kindness to others. In which aspect of your life can you show yourself more kindness?

_____

_____

_____

_____

_____

_____

_____

_____

_____

_____

_____

_____

_____

_____

Day 36

Taking responsibility is a stepping-stone in your healing process. It's a vital step that cannot be skipped. The majority of empowerment comes through the ability to take responsibility for your future, to reclaim your motivation and your ability to live life to the fullest.

Taking personal responsibility means taking charge of your life and your emotional state! It's a powerful step to take and one that can ultimately set you free.

Note to myself   Date _____

In which aspect of your life have you stopped taking control of? How can you turn that around today and get back in the driver's seat of your life?

_____

_____

_____

_____

_____

_____

_____

_____

_____

_____

Day 37

Be strong, stand firm, and believe in yourself and your ability to move forward in life, despite the convictions and lack of belief that others have in you. What ultimately matters is how much you believe in yourself.

Sometimes people give their power away to an ailment or authority figure. When a person takes responsibility for him or herself, they take away control that circumstances have over them.

Note to myself   Date _____

Who in your life or past do you need to take your power back from?

_____

_____

_____

_____

_____

_____

_____

_____

_____

_____

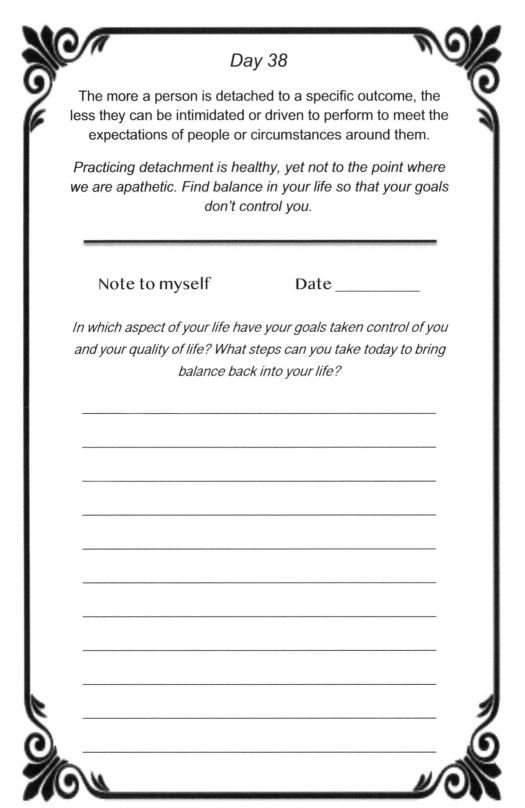

Day 38

The more a person is detached to a specific outcome, the less they can be intimidated or driven to perform to meet the expectations of people or circumstances around them.

Practicing detachment is healthy, yet not to the point where we are apathetic. Find balance in your life so that your goals don't control you.

Note to myself   Date _____

In which aspect of your life have your goals taken control of you and your quality of life? What steps can you take today to bring balance back into your life?

_____

_____

_____

_____

_____

_____

_____

_____

_____

_____

_____

Day 39

Letting of unhealthy circumstances comes naturally once the story from the past is understood.

To be able to move forward and away from a challenging past does not always mean you have to forgive. Moving forward does mean that you no longer desperately cling to grudges and trauma anymore. It means you can move forward and away from problems that held you back and most importantly of letting go of the past. In this instance, letting go is accompanied by a sense of peace and understanding.

Letting go is to understand your actions and reactions to circumstances and the behavior of another.

Note to myself   Date _____

You are probably asking, "How does a person move forward from an incident that tipped their life upside down?". The first step is to identify the pain and issue or issues that you're holding on to. Sometimes you might just feel angry and resentful without really understanding why. From whom or what is your anger or resentment keeping you safe from? Has your anger now started to serve you as a psychological boundary? How can you implement healthier boundaries in your life today?

_____

_____

_____

_____

Day 40

Life is not a competition but a platform to grow, embrace this process!

We never stop growing; we never stop learning. Allow yourself sometimes to be a student.

Note to myself   Date _____

What new skill or behavior can you learn or adapt to that will bring more positive changes into your personal life today?

_____

_____

_____

_____

_____

_____

_____

_____

_____

_____

_____

_____

_____

Day 41

We become so attached to who we have become as a result of our past, as this false identity is all that we know.

How high is the price that you are paying for this false identity? Change in the short term can sometimes be just as difficult as holding onto your false identity, which could result in a lifetime of pain.

Note to myself   Date _____

What can you do differently today that would allow authentic aspects of your true identity to gently surface today?

_____

_____

_____

_____

_____

_____

_____

_____

_____

_____

_____

_____

Day 42

When there is a need, there is a purpose waiting to be fulfilled.

No one in life is without a purpose; we all contribute in our own way. There are no big or small purposes.

Note to myself   Date _____

You can already be serving multiple purposes without realizing it. Which positive attributes and talents have you undermined recently? What stops you from nurturing those aspects more in your daily life?

_____

_____

_____

_____

_____

_____

_____

_____

_____

_____

_____

Day 43

Always be true to yourself and others. A facade gives you false confidence and leads to false and misdirected intentions.

It gives the illusion that one is healed and making progress, but the progress made comes at a price. When you move forward in life with your baggage intact, you will inevitably disappoint others and fail to meet your expectations.

Note to myself   Date _____

In which area of your life has your false identity or coping mechanisms given you false confidence? Which healthy habits do you need to implement to know and believe that you no longer need a false identity?

_____

_____

_____

_____

_____

_____

_____

_____

_____

_____

Day 44

Emotions are an expression and an echo of old pain. Fears are an expression of complex emotions that cannot be translated by the heart.

Life is like an emotional rollercoaster. There are scary times, happy times, and moments of depression. Never blame yourself for feeling a negative emotion, however, be mindful of not giving that emotion the power to rob you of your quality of life.

Note to myself   Date _____

Which negative emotion has become dominant in your life? What is the opposite feeling of this emotion? What can you differently today in order to access and feel that positive emotion?

_____

_____

_____

_____

_____

_____

_____

_____

_____

_____

Day 45

Emotional responses occur not by conscious choice but also by disposition and past stress and trauma.

As humans with an intellectual brain, we can master and control our emotions, instead of being controlled by them. I invite you to playfully challenge yourself today to take charge of how you feel, especially if you feel stuck with negative emotions.

Note to myself   Date _____

Just because you presently feel a negative emotion doesn't mean that the cause of it is still real and present in your life. Sometimes current circumstances can trigger old pain. Be in a state of awareness today.

_____

_____

_____

_____

_____

_____

_____

_____

_____

Day 46

You create your reality…. well sort of…your reality creates you. Space holds matter and matter defines your reality.

You perceive your reality, and as a result of your perception, you experience emotions and thoughts shared by collective consciousness and biological responses. You then intellectually create your reality by the way you perceive it and the way it makes you feel based on your experiences. You feel your emotions as a result of your reality activating predisposed emotions related to ancestral experiences as well as your own.

Note to myself   Date _____

What mindset do you need to hold today in order experience your life from a new, healthy and fresh perspective?

_____

_____

_____

_____

_____

_____

_____

_____

_____

_____

Day 47

Forgiveness means moving on, in whatever capacity you can. Always remember that forgiveness = empowerment, and freedom.

Forgiveness takes time, be kind to yourself. You will let go. The day will come. This too shall pass.

Note to myself   Date _____

What is your definition of forgiveness?

_____

_____

_____

_____

_____

_____

_____

_____

_____

_____

_____

_____

_____

Day 48

When you intend to serve a purpose, that is when your purpose will begin to serve you.

When you start a goal or set a plan in motion, make sure that you are beginning this goal with a positive attitude and the right support.

Note to myself   Date _____

The initial energy that a goal is created from will become the foundation of that goal and how it plays out. What kind of mindset are you going to nurture today when you start a goal?

_____

_____

_____

_____

_____

_____

_____

_____

_____

_____

_____

_____

Day 49

When all your efforts fail, remember that you are the only actor on stage in your life, everyone else is part of the audience.

Keep your head up high today, keep dancing, take the lead, and make your performance a damn good show!

_____

Note to myself   Date _____

What can you do differently today in order to be more playful when you are faced with a challenge?

_____

_____

_____

_____

_____

_____

_____

_____

_____

_____

_____

_____

_____

Day 50

Understanding how the body operates can be challenging.

People become depressed when they disconnect from their true passion in life and when they allow others to tell them what to do. They become even more depressed when they feel disconnected from their bodies unable to understand that their symptoms are caused by the body's natural responses to unresolved conflict and pain.

If your body is in pain, or if something feels wrong, then imagine that this specific area in your body that you feel concerned about has a voice. If it could speak, what would it say?

Note to myself   Date _____

Give your body a voice and allow it to speak. It will tell you what the emotional stress is behind the physical problem. Meditate, start listening and takes notes. I invite you to start today.

_____

_____

_____

_____

_____

_____

_____

_____

Day 51

When your self-worth was questioned or challenged, then it will be more vulnerable to the manipulation of influential people. It's time to find yourself and reclaim your power.

Never give your power away to people you perceive as an authority figure. Because someone might have more status than you do not mean that it gives them the right to abuse or undermine you.

Note to myself   Date _____

What do you need to believe in yourself in order to know that are worthy of love and respect?

_____

_____

_____

_____

_____

_____

_____

_____

_____

_____

_____

_____

Day 52

Is one really suffering from depression or are doctors too lazy to listen to the symptoms, which may indicate that something else is wrong?

Are artificial coping substances always the answer, or does a person need a good listener sometimes? There are cases where someone genuinely suffers from a chemical imbalance. However, it is sometimes the case that people are misdiagnosed and are given mediation, which temporarily resolves an issue, only to create another medical problem due to the toxicity in the medication.

Note to myself

Date _____

Do you have an unhealthy coping mechanism such as overusing substances? What does the coping mechanism make you feel that you cannot feel and access on your own? How are you standing in your own way that could be preventing you from stepping into the full essence of this positive emotion that is being blocked?

_____

_____

_____

_____

_____

_____

_____

Day 53

People's lives are based on a series of events: their upbringing, trauma / stress or ancestral trauma and patterns.

You are an expression of your ancestors, and your life experiences can switch this predisposition to trauma/medical/psychological patterns on or off.

_____

Note to myself   Date _____

Which inherited pattern/s do you have that you are aware of? What can you do differently in order to embrace your true authentic self today?

_____
_____
_____
_____
_____
_____
_____
_____
_____
_____
_____

Day 54

When people move away from their authentic self and their goals, their body becomes rigid, resistant, fatigued, or depressed. It dims your light and passion for life.

Sometimes you cannot change your circumstances due to responsibilities. You can, however, change how you feel about those circumstances.

Note to myself   Date _____

When you make a change in your thought patterns you are taking control back and are moving back into the driver's seat of your life. What would the emotional benefits be if you take control back and become more flexible with yourself today?

_____

_____

_____

_____

_____

_____

_____

_____

_____

_____

_____

_____

Day 55

People respond to circumstances, their environment, and the people around them based on their past and ancestral trauma. There is a hidden code that drives our emotional responses.

Your life becomes stressful when you cannot pinpoint the origin of your emotions and the trauma that triggered them. It's even more frustrating to be on the receiving end of someone else's confusion by not understanding how they feel or even why they feel the way that they do. Practice patience today.

Note to myself   Date _____

In which aspect of your life can you practice more patience today?

_____

_____

_____

_____

_____

_____

_____

_____

_____

_____

Day 56

Our lives are influenced and directed by past trauma and stressful events.

People make decisions based on past trauma and negative experiences without even realizing it.

Note to myself   Date _____

Become aware today why you make certain decisions, especially if you felt hesitant to make a recent decision. It can be a result of your intuition trying to send you a message or it could be a result of an old memory that was triggered, causing you to feel confused in terms of what to do and how to respond. Take a minute, be silent and follow the trail of emotions and inner voices that are in conflict.

_____

_____

_____

_____

_____

_____

_____

_____

_____

_____

Day 57

Your past is now a story, and your future is untold.

Note to myself   Date _____

What can you do differently today to get the most out of the present moment?

_____

_____

_____

_____

_____

_____

_____

_____

_____

_____

_____

_____

_____

_____

_____

_____

_____

_____

Day 58

When you are able to change how you feel about your life and learn how to manifest your goals, despite your challenges and circumstances, this is when your true authentic inner power will surface.

Note to myself   Date _____

There will be times in life when you are trying to achieve a goal, only to find yourself with no support and no compassion. Never stop believing in yourself, become your own best cheerleader! How can you be more focused on your needs today?

_____

_____

_____

_____

_____

_____

_____

_____

_____

_____

_____

_____

Day 59

Many people are stuck in a fight or flight instinct as a result of abuse, rejection, or abandonment trauma. They found a survival tool/skill that helped them to cope with trauma in their lives.

The negative circumstances may have ended however, their coping or survival pattern doesn't. As you change and heal, so should your coping skills. These skills served you during a time that may not exist anymore. These coping mechanisms will only cause you to live in the past and prevent you from moving forward.

Note to myself   Date _____

As you change, so should your survival strategies. Actions and reactions that served you in the past might inevitably destroy what you are trying build for your future. Be more mindful of your behavior, patterns, actions and reactions so that they are in alignment with your goals, dreams and future.

_____

_____

_____

_____

_____

_____

_____

_____

Day60

Trauma, conflict in values, conflict in belief systems, and emotional needs are mainly responsible for our problems as a human race.

I invite you today to be mindful of another's belief system, values, and emotional needs, without having to sacrifice any aspect of yourself and your self-worth.

Note to myself   Date _____

Observe and become aware today how your values are in conflict with someone else's. Become aware of how you manage conflict. How do you react? Do you retreat? Do you respond by trying to impose your point of view? Are you trying to change the other person's opinion because you feel that you are right, and they are wrong? How judgmental are you? Is the circumstance that you might find yourself in worth the energy that you invest in it to prove yourself, right? Learn to be more accepting and tolerant today without having or needing to change anything about the other person's value, belief system or opinion

_____

_____

_____

_____

_____

_____

_____

Day 61

Your boundaries are influenced by past trauma.

If you were punished in the past for saying "no," then this may affect whether or not you feel worthy of saying "no" now. Instead of exercising and establishing healthy boundaries, people draw their power and boundaries from their anger, or they retreat and become invisible.

Note to myself   Date _____

Boundaries can be established with firmness, yet also with love. If you were disciplined in an aggressive way during your childhood, then it could set a pattern for how you deal with your own boundaries and how you express them. The good news is that you can change how you express your boundaries. You can control how others treat you by expressing your boundaries. The first step is to be clear about what your boundaries are. Where is your threshold. What will you accept and what will you not accept? Remember that by the time you feel resentful toward someone, it means that your boundaries have been overstepped a long time ago. Learn to recognize where that fine line is. That is your homeplay for today. Define what your boundaries are. What will you accept and what will you not accept? Most important of all is respect yourself enough to respect your boundaries

_____

_____

_____

_____

Day 62

What you learn and observe during your childhood becomes a big part of your life's foundation. This effects how you behave and respond to others and the environment around you.

Note to myself   Date _____

As an adult you have the power to radically change your life, how you show up, how you act and react. Your identity is not tied down to your past. Who you are is so much more than just your past. What can you do differently to give yourself the love and attention that you need and desire?

_____

_____

_____

_____

_____

_____

_____

_____

_____

_____

_____

_____

Day 63

Most people have suffered from some stressful event, in one form or another.

This can lead to feelings of discouragement, fear of making changes in life as you start to feel comfortable feeling uncomfortable. It will never feel like the right time to leap to change and move on. Now is the time!

Note to myself   Date _____

You may unknowingly be holding onto old stress as a reminder of how circumstances and people have caused you hurt and betrayal. This is called an unconscious secondary gain. I invite you today to come to the gentle realization that the strategies that served you in the past might actually be sabotaging your happiness right now and holding you back. Your past is now in the past, let it stay there. Your actions and reactions that served you in the past, might not serve today. Become aware of how your life has changed, how YOU have changed and make sure that your actions and reactions are in alignment with your present life. Your baggage will not lead you to success.

_____

_____

_____

_____

_____

_____

_____

Day 64

When you hold on to your pain because it has become a trophy and represents your life story, it has become your false identity.

Who you are is not your past. You are not a victim; you are a survivor! Who you are is part of God, and part of a much bigger plan. You expand into eternity and are loved and appreciated with so much depth and passion. Your past circumstances can cause changes in your characteristics, but even that can be healed and changed, which will ultimately lead you back to your true authentic self!

Note to myself   Date _____

In which aspect of your life have you neglected your authentic characteristics within you?

_____

_____

_____

_____

_____

_____

_____

_____

_____

Day 65

When you have had a challenging past, it can be difficult to come to grips with the after-effects thereof.

The more you deny how you truly feel about your past, the more your body will suffer and shout out to you in the form of psychological and medical conditions. When you have experienced a challenging time, then it's essential to reach out for support. It is not the wisest decision to try and combat pain on your own. You are worthy and deserving of support. Often a big block that we have is that we don't trust, especially any kind of support, as support might have come at a price in the past or you were obligated to return a favor. This can be resolved with clear communication and exercising healthy boundaries.

Note to myself   Date _____

In which aspect of your life do you need more support and clearer boundaries?

_____

_____

_____

_____

_____

_____

_____

_____

Day 66

What was once an emotional issue can change into a physical issue.

It is so important that we understand the language of our bodies. Our body is communicating and talking to us every single day. Often we ignore it or try to silence it by drinking alcohol or abusing substances. Your body will never fail you; it will always do it's best to survive and to help you survive. However, if we keep missing our bodies cry for help and need for attention, we will inevitably pay with pain.

Note to myself   Date _____

Once your body has exhausted all the resources it has to cope with a challenge that it's facing, that is when medical conditions start to surface. Learn to meditate and listen to what your body want and need, it is after all here to serve you. How can you serve your body today so that this pattern can become a daily routine?

_____

_____

_____

_____

_____

_____

_____

_____

Day 67

If you only address the symptoms of your problems and not the original cause, then you might find that you attract circumstances and people that trigger your deepest and most vulnerable feelings.

Emotions that you perhaps thought you had put behind you might resurface in an even more intense and disabling way. We all have found ourselves in a place in our life where we thought we had dealt with an emotionally challenging issue, just to find out that we didn't even scratch the surface of it. That is okay; it doesn't mean that you did something wrong or that you missed something either. We all heal at our own pace.

Note to myself   Date _____

Where in your life have you been too hard on yourself and your healing journey?

_____

_____

_____

_____

_____

_____

_____

_____

Day 68

Becoming aware of one's problems and the reason why they are there is life-changing!

It's the beginning of a powerful healing journey. Awareness is what sets healing in motion!

Note to myself   Date _____

Which problematic situation in your life have you ignored for far too long? What in your life will change that you are not ready to change if you did start to address it today?

_____

_____

_____

_____

_____

_____

_____

_____

_____

_____

_____

_____

_____

Day 69

Being in control of your own life is a very powerful state of mind to be in. People have given away their power to authority, aggressors, and circumstances.

It's easier to give in to others than to take ownership. It's called taking responsibility.

Note to myself   Date _____

This was a big lesson for me personally. I also have to add that people often feel ashamed when they are confronted with circumstances that point out that they have been avoiding responsibility and failed at something as a result. It's easier to blame and become angry in order to deflect from seeing your own mistakes. I have been there, and it's not a great place or frame of mind to be in. What is important, though, is to let go of the shame. Become aware of where your weaknesses lie and make changes where and when needed. Being responsible for yourself and your future can be a heavy burden to carry, especially if you have been burned out in the past by being too responsible and taking responsibility where you should not have.

Or you took responsibility for someone else's pain, goals or future outcome. Ultimately you are responsible for yourself – if you are a parent, then it's a given that you are responsible for your child, but I am keeping it on a broader context for now. Be clear where your true responsibilities lie. Also have clear boundaries and know when you need to take a step back or take a step into circumstances. Practice discernment today.

Day 70

Wishing is a great way to envision what you want. Your will power will transform a wish into reality!

If there is a will, there is a way! The secret is to stay focused, be loyal to your goals, and never allow someone to sway you from path!

Note to myself   Date _____

Keep moving forward despite any challenges that might come your way. Success will be yours! What do you need to believe in yourself in order to know that you can overcome your challenges today?

_____

_____

_____

_____

_____

_____

_____

_____

_____

_____

_____

Day 71

My intention for you: One of the purposes of my work is to empower you to be more aware of how the body feels and what it may be trying to tell you.

I want to remind you how to listen to your body, to understand your trauma, to understand emotional and physical blocks.

Note to myself   Date _____

I invite you today, to change your most dominant negative thought to "I can heal and change gracefully"

_____

_____

_____

_____

_____

_____

_____

_____

_____

_____

_____

_____

_____

Day 72

We don't need anything outside of ourselves to grow emotionally and spiritually.

All emotional resources are at your fingertips, just waiting to be tapped into. You are a walking miracle. Everything that you could need to live a fantastic life and attract what you want is already right there inside of you. These beautiful resources are an extension of your genetic line, your ancestry! These resources are blocked by stress. The only thing that is standing between you and your resources is your willingness to let go of what no longer serves you.

Note to myself   Date _____

Your mind and energy is unconscious, so invested in holding onto the past that it robs you of the clarity and peace of mind that you need in order to access powerful resources. Which positive emotion can you focus on today to greatly improve your happiness and quality of life?

_____

_____

_____

_____

_____

_____

_____

_____

Day 73

You will often hold on to survival skills that were unconsciously formed during stressful times and these coping skills can either have a positive or negative effect on your life and future.

You may often get caught in a flight or fight state of mind, depending on which instinctive response served you during a challenging time. What also happens is that often this instinctive response does not reset itself after the challenge or danger has passed. Many people live in this flight or fight state.

Note to myself   Date _____

This state of mind will only rob you of your quality of life and your ability to make healthy and sound decisions as your judgment can be influenced by past experiences that are no longer real, yet it has a negative impact on your ability to gracefully move forward and make healthy decisions. In which aspect of your life could you still be playing out old coping mechanisms?

_____

_____

_____

_____

_____

_____

_____

_____

Day 74

When have you sacrificed your values and what was once important to you for the sake of acceptance and to fit in?

When have you abandoned love to achieve superficial goals that took you away from your true authentic self and purpose?

Note to myself   Date _____

In which aspect of your life have you stopped being true to your goals and needs?

_____

_____

_____

_____

_____

_____

_____

_____

_____

_____

_____

_____

_____

Day 75

Life is not always easy, but when you look at the bigger picture, what exactly are you comparing it with?

Life will have its ups and downs. How we react during these times will determine our experience.

Note to myself   Date _____

Where in your life are you perhaps reacting too little or overreacting?

_____

_____

_____

_____

_____

_____

_____

_____

_____

_____

_____

_____

_____

_____

_____

Day 76

Your chances of success do not lie in your job or position as a parent, friend, or colleague. It is within you. You can be in a high-profile role, but that doesn't mean that you feel successful or accomplished. You might feel overburdened, stressed, and find yourself short of time. This could be driven by fear of failure, causing you to think that you have to work harder than what is needed. Or perhaps you are still trying to prove someone wrong. Success is when you feel accomplished in your goals; you know that your efforts are good enough. You no longer evaluate your success based on how much you can do and how good you can do it.

Note to myself   Date _____

Where in your life do you feel truly accomplished? What can you do differently to bring more flow and success into this area of your life?

_____

_____

_____

_____

_____

_____

_____

_____

_____

Day 77

People who have become too competitive live their lives with lack of playful choices; they live only to win and survive.

Remember that you always have choices in life. You choose how you reach your destination; you decide how you are going to feel and respond to circumstances and people in your life. When you make a decision, it takes discipline and willpower to see it through to the end, but what is important is not to lose sight of the reason and motivation you had in the beginning to execute the decision you made.

Note to myself   Date _____

Stay true to yourself, be kind to others and make sure that your goals are in alignment with your true authentic self. What action can you take today to be more in alignment with your goals?

_____

_____

_____

_____

_____

_____

_____

_____

_____

_____

Day 78

The science of epigenetics: The science of epigenetics demonstrates that trauma creates biological change, which can last for many generations.

That means trauma that people experience, even just witnessing it, can create physical and emotional changes to their future grandchildren and great-grandchildren.

Note to myself   Date _____

Which inherited traits of your mother and father are you expressing? List the negative aspects and then write down the opposite action or emotion. What can you do differently today In order to allow yourself to tap more into the opposite positive aspects?

_____

_____

_____

_____

_____

_____

_____

_____

_____

_____

Day 79

Today is me, myself, and I day. Just be YOU! Be who you truly want to be. The people who love you will love you for it.

The people who don't will fall away. It's called spiritual detox!

Note to myself   Date _____

Give yourself permission today to just be you and stop trying to be like a square block squeezing through a triangular hole! When you are expressing your true authentic self you are being honest and true to not only yourself, but to other people as well. Give yourself the gift of freedom today and allow this to be the start of an amazing journey! Rediscover your identity and who you truly want to be!

_____

_____

_____

_____

_____

_____

_____

_____

_____

Day 80

Amongst many symptoms, unresolved stress creates a barrier around a person, causing them to push others away.

As a result of old stressful events, a person establishes boundaries with this barrier, which is often anger or by wanting to hide.

Stress can have an enormous impact on a person's physical and psychological health.

Often what happens when a person experiences a great deal of stress, and they felt out of control of the situation could form unhealthy coping mechanisms.

As a result, depending on which instinctive response served this person, let's say the fight instinct kept them safe and helped them to survive, then they will associate their boundaries with anger.

Note to myself   Date _____

As a result, when this person need to say no or express a boundary, a great deal of anger might be triggered and be expressed in a way that might be out of alignment with the given circumstances at hand. I invite you today to become aware of how you react during the day. When you need to say no or express a boundary, do you hide or do you become passive or aggressive? Do you feel you have to fight for your boundaries or do you become the peacekeeper? Be an observer today.

_____

_____

_____

Day 81

Symptoms of stress are the initial complaint of the problem that has surfaced as a result of the trauma or stress. This is the starting point of your healing process.

There are many layers to symptoms of stress. What is essential is that the cause of the stress is dealt with and not just the symptoms. Suppressing the symptoms with alcohol or abusing substances will only prolong a much-needed healing journey. Love yourself enough to take that leap and give yourself the biggest gift that you possibly can…. a gift of emotional freedom!

Note to myself   Date _____

What is your biggest complaint today? What can you change in your life or thought process today in order to take your power back and bring more balance you're your life?

_____

_____

_____

_____

_____

_____

_____

_____

_____

Day 82

I invite you today to 100% believe in the person that you want to become, which ultimately is the person that you already are! You have to remember what it felt like!

Your inner resources are powerful beyond measure. You can be who you want to be. Wanting to be like someone else means you are rejecting yourself. No one can love themselves and want to become something that they are not intended to be. If you have always dreamed of being like someone else, then you would have been them in this life. Have role models, but don't compare yourself to others; they might not have the talents, love, friendships; and gifts that you have.

_____

Note to myself   Date _____

You are always blessed and there is always something in your life to be grateful for, even during the rainy days. What are you grateful for today?

_____
_____
_____
_____
_____
_____
_____

Day 83

A traumatic experience may be imprinted and stored in the brain. There is suppressed adrenaline in the body, and the muscles are still tense, as if though the body still wants to protect itself from a possible threat.

This behavior surfaces as tension and rigidity. This is why certain past traumas can create so many long-term symptoms in the human body. If the human body was designed to hold onto stress for long periods of time, or be in stressful circumstances for long periods of time, then why are we faced with so many medical conditions? Our core imprint is meant to be harmonious.

Note to myself   Date _____

To be in harmony with one another, have peace of mind, to be in sync with life and the journey we are accomplishing. In which area of your life have you become too rigid? How can you be more playful today?

_____

_____

_____

_____

_____

_____

_____

_____

Day 84

When you are addressing and recovering from an injury, the sooner you deal with it, the better the results are physically and emotionally.

It is essential to deal with physical injuries before the secondary gain patterns set in! We all have secondary gains in life; often we benefit from something that is unhealthy or bad for us. It can be the same with physical injuries. Usually a person might not heal as they are receiving the love and care that they have been longing for. Or they finally see people in their lives again that they have missed for a long time. If they heal all this love and attention might leave their lives.

Note to myself   Date _____

Become aware today if you have someone like that in your life if you have had this pattern in the past or unconsciously even still have it. Know that you are worthy and deserving of having the love and care that you want and need in this life! But love has to start with you, it has to start within.

_____
_____
_____
_____
_____
_____

Day 85

Stress is a significant cause of disease and psychological stress, which we have trouble healing. Any successful healing tool should enable you to resolve your stress in a non-stressful way.

Healing your life should not have to be painful or traumatize you again in any way. Always remember to be gentle with yourself. Nurture yourself when you are going through a healing process. Let go of any shame that you feel when you take time out for yourself.

Note to myself   Date _____

If you don't look after yourself then you are making yourself less powerful and less able to help and support others. You have to be there for yourself first!

_____

_____

_____

_____

_____

_____

_____

_____

_____

_____

Day 86

Why some people don't heal: In a moment of a stressful situation, you will find a way to be and feel safe.

This may include reaching out to someone for safety or taking comfort in numbness or the freeze instinct. Every time you experience a similar trauma or stressful event, you may revert to the state of mind and gut instinct that kept you safe initially. Often people don't fully heal from a stressful event. It is so important to remember that you didn't do anything wrong; neither did you miss anything. Your body and unconscious mind are trying to keep you safe.

Note to myself   Date _____

There is a pattern that kept you safe in the past and your instinctive responses are still holding on to this pattern and way of reacting to stress to keep you safe, as it served you in the past. What is your default coping mechanism? What can you replace it with that is healthier for you?

_____

_____

_____

_____

_____

_____

_____

_____

Day 87

Feeling numb or feeling paralyzed may once have positively served you at some point in your life.

This positive survival tactic has negative consequences. The numbness will influence every aspect of your life, including emotionally dissociating from your environment. Ever wondered why you are emotionally unavailable to people or in relationships? Why you can't emotionally connect or even relate to people in your life?

Note to myself   Date _____

What is your biggest fear regarding today's quote? What can you do more of in your life in order to reignite your inner power and confidence?

_____

_____

_____

_____

_____

_____

_____

_____

_____

_____

Day 88

Often, we are so attached to what we want that we have become blind to what we already have. Our entire life can pass by us. Don't leave room in your life for regret.

Invest in what you know is realistic for you. Never give up on your goals and your vision for the future. Just make sure that what you desire is coming from a positive mindset. Make sure that you are not sacrificing your energy and quality of life in your pursuit for success just because you are trying to prove someone wrong or prove that you are worthy.

Note to myself   Date _____

Success does not define who you are as a person. Which positive qualities do you have that defines your character?

_____

_____

_____

_____

_____

_____

_____

_____

_____

Day 89

Never base your self-worth on the external world or on how others treat you.

Often people project their issues onto you, and you should never take it personally. We are all responsible for what we choose to carry in life and if that burden becomes too heavy, then it should never be used as an excuse to hurt another.

Note to myself   Date _____

Breathe in love and exhale love.

_____

_____

_____

_____

_____

_____

_____

_____

_____

_____

_____

Day 90

Your pain is not your protection shield. The problem starts when you hold on to hurt from the past. You might think that it will protect you from future events that might be painful.

Living in the past will not give you the freedom that you need. Remember that what your resist will persist. By letting go of how past experiences have made you feel could be the greatest gift and ticket to emotional and psychological freedom! I invite you today to entertain the idea that you will be happier and healthier in life without the baggage of your past.

Note to myself   Date _____

You don't need pain in order to stay safe. What you do need is healthy boundaries and support. Be open to that today. How can you be more open to being supported and express healthy boundaries?

_____

_____

_____

_____

_____

_____

_____

_____

_____

Day 91

People often establish boundaries based on past negative experiences when boundaries were overstepped, or a voice was suppressed.

You might fear that letting go of a stressful situation that challenged your boundaries in the past would weaken your ability to stand up for yourself in the future. Also, you might fear to let go, as you are so familiar with the negative state of mind that it has left you with

Note to myself   Date _____

Know that no long-term positive results can be manifested from anger, pain and scarcity. What is your deep underlying intention when you want to start a goal?

_____

_____

_____

_____

_____

_____

_____

_____

_____

_____

Day 92

Do you have a fear of change? Familiarity often overpowers common logic.

Change is not always a pleasant process. Especially if you have a negative association with it, meaning things still went wrong when you were going through changes; this could either be emotional changes, growth, or changes in your environment. Any change in circumstances may cause you to feel unsafe and stressed. Often, people learn to feel comfortable with feeling uncomfortable as a person they might not always know how to survive or emotionally cope in a new set of circumstances without support or guidance.

Note to myself   Date _____

One of many possibilities could be that a person was too controlled or smothered during their childhood. I invite you today to have fun with change! Make small changes here and there and then start making bigger changes when you feel ready. The secret is to HAVE FUN and be creative!

_____

_____

_____

_____

_____

_____

_____

Day 93

Did you know that in many cases, the original trauma that has affected a person may have occurred before their birth?

Or it may relate to their time in the womb or at conception. People may even be expressing unresolved biological trauma from their grandparents and ancestors. You are an expression of your ancestry. Predisposition trauma, illnesses, and unresolved traumas that your ancestors experienced are lying dormant in your genetic make-up.

Note to myself   Date _____

Stress in your external world can cause these predisposed trauma or illnesses and unresolved traumas to surface! Which coping mechanisms do you share with a parent or grandparent? Is this strategy healthy or unhealthy for you? You can transform it by having awareness of your reactions today and consciously choosing a new reaction.

_____

_____

_____

_____

_____

_____

_____

Day 94

A dissociative state is rarely permanent. This dissociative state creates a new route (or neural pathway) around a traumatic memory to suppress it.

This allows you to deal with day-to-day situations without feeling the negative symptoms associated with a stressful event from the past or present circumstances. Numbing yourself from your past is not going to give you the quality of life that you want or truly deserve. Letting go of the numbness does not mean that you will experience the pain from the past again. Numbness does not equal inner strength; it means that you are avoiding letting go and stepping into your power. A gentle way to approach this and to start making changes by resolving your lack of self-worth and to strengthen your boundaries.

Note to myself   Date _____

Letting go of the past might be more rewarding than what you could ever have imagined! Be open to a new way of life. What can you embrace today that would allow you to be open to a new healthier life?

_____

_____

_____

_____

_____

Day 95

You deserve the love that you give just as much as those who are receiving it! You are only as worthy as another. Why should you have to pull the short end of the rope? Why should you have to sacrifice your needs for the sake of another?

Who told you that you are not allowed to be loved as deeply as you love others? Let go, delete and dismiss any old lingering negative thoughts and voices.

Note to myself   Date _____

I invite you today to allow yourself to receive the love that you give!

_____
_____
_____
_____
_____
_____
_____
_____
_____
_____
_____

Day 96

When old trauma is reactivated, it can cause you to feel overwhelmed by past pain. The thought of "Haven't I already worked on this?" begin to resurface.

This magnifies any depression and anxiety. Your dissociative state has served its purpose. It is your body's way of nudging you forward to finally let go of that last piece! It's time to heal. Instead of feeling upset when emotional blocks that you worked on in the past resurface, see this as an opportunity to delve even deeper into the core issue that is holding you back. Remember your body will always try to protect you. Often, the body will release stress in phases and that it feels ready.

Note to myself   Date _____

I invite you today to trust your body and trust the process that is unfolding. If you feel blocked, what can you do for yourself that would allow you to feel more supported and nurtured?

_____

_____

_____

_____

_____

_____

_____

_____

Day 97

When plan number 1 fails, breathe, act cool, keep calm, and carry on. There are a trillion more numbers!

Failure is an experience that we ALL have been through, I am not new to it, and neither are you. What successful people remember is the passion that drove them to try again and again! Remember why you started the goal that you had in the first place. Go back to the drawing board and be flexible with your methods!

Note to myself   Date _____

When you feel stuck today in your personal life or business, what steps can you take to be more creative and playful with your approaches?

_____

_____

_____

_____

_____

_____

_____

_____

_____

_____

Day 98

Fun Fact: Survival instincts are behavior patterns that keep people alive. What makes an instinct become a survival instinct is that it directly and immediately leads to a person's survival.

Survival instincts are also called 'animal instincts' because they relate to base animal responses – something that all animals, or at least all vertebrates (fish, birds, reptiles, and mammals), share.

Note to myself   Date _____

What is your most dominant instinctive response when you are faced with a challenge?

_____

_____

_____

_____

_____

_____

_____

_____

_____

_____

Day 99

When you experience a stressful event, in most cases you dissociate from it.

This may create a sensation as if the stressful event never happened, or that it no longer affects you. Stress is suppressed, leaving confusion and debilitating symptoms behind. Ignoring how an event or person made you feel will only hold you back from claiming the love and life that you truly deserve. Remember when you experienced an event that was not stressful to you however, it might have been for someone else, it's important to explore whether you just dissociated from the event.

Note to myself   Date _____

This means that what you experienced is still in your unconscious mind and an event in the future could potentially activate suppressed emotions. Your body is like a cup. It can only handle a certain amount until it starts to overflow. Be kind to yourself. Even the strongest people have their vulnerable moments.

_____

_____

_____

_____

_____

_____

Day 100

We all have people who gossip about us behind our backs.

I invite you to be OK with this, they are behind your back and not in front of you for a reason. Keep your head high, never feel that you have to change yourself in order to be accepted by another. People gossip about you because they live in a world of judgment. They are expressing their pain and self-rejection by trying to expose yours. Often people need to belittle others so that they can feel better about themselves.

Note to myself   Date _____

You no longer have to accept this type of behavior. You deserve friends and people in your life who will hold you in the highest regard. In which area of your life are you undermining your worth as a partner, friend or colleague?

_____

_____

_____

_____

_____

_____

_____

_____

_____

_____

Day 101

Failure is not an option; a different method to move forward again is what's needed!

Failure doesn't mean losing, although people can take it hard, and I have as well in the past. Be graceful when something you planned or worked toward didn't work out. Successful people who are out there have achieved their dreams because they never gave up.

Note to myself   Date _____

In which area of your life have you given up? What do you need to believe in yourself in order to know that you can make a success of it?

_____

_____

_____

_____

_____

_____

_____

_____

_____

_____

_____

Day 102

Problems are not there to sabotage your progress. They arrive to show you an alternative route that might end up being better than the one you had planned.

Sometimes we have to give the universe a chance and allow it to help guide us in the direction that we are meant to be heading in. Be flexible and be open to new methods and possibilities.

Note to myself   Date _____

How can you be more open to new methods and possibilities today? What kind of mind set do you need to have throughout the day in order to become aware of new methods and possibilities in your relationships, work or friendships?

_____

_____

_____

_____

_____

_____

_____

_____

_____

Day 103

Do you have selective hearing? Selective hearing surfaces when an unresolved trauma comes up while you are trying to resolve and heal an emotional issue. You may have signs of selective hearing.

Selective hearing is when you can't hear everything that is being said by a practitioner or person who is trying to help you. Instead, you find yourself focusing on hearing only selective words, in an attempt to avoid hearing the truth.

Note to myself   Date _____

There are times when someone might say something that triggers an unpleasant memory in the back of your mind that unconsciously prevented you from hearing certain words, which as a result impacted what you thought you heard. Who in your life do you feel you are blocking when they are expressing themselves. What is the worst thing that can happen if you allowed yourself to truly listen to their truth?

_____

_____

_____

_____

_____

_____

_____

Day 104

When you suppress stress; it will surface in different ways until your body has found a way to release the tension. Once this cycle is complete, the memory of the stress becomes like a foreign, distant memory, and the symptoms will subside.

Your body needs an outlet when it has experienced shock or trauma. As humans, we have suppressed our natural ability to process shock and stress. As a result, the stress piles up in the body and if the issue or emotional stress is not addressed, then often, medical conditions can surface. Love your body and listen to it when it tries to communicate with you.

Note to myself   Date _____

Your body is here to serve you, nurture it so that it can work with you to achieve your goals. How can you best serve your physical body today?

_____

_____

_____

_____

_____

_____

_____

_____

Day 105

A healing crisis may start when too much stress has been suppressed to such an extent that you cannot identify with your new sense of self without your old fear.

This indicates that the hidden benefits of the trauma (also called secondary gain) have not been addressed. We all have been on a healing journey in one way or another. It doesn't always require energy or any kind of healing modality. It takes place by experiencing true love and hearing sincere, kind words, to name a few. We feel better, for a while, only to find ourselves having a relapse and feeling old negative emotions and patterns resurfacing again.

Note to myself   Date _____

I invite you to ask yourself today, what is the benefit of this old emotion or pattern that has been weighing you down recently? Who can you become if you set yourself from free from this?

_____

_____

_____

_____

_____

_____

_____

_____

Day 106

Your entire life may have been based on and driven by predisposed trauma. Once the trauma has been released, it is like starting a new chapter in your life.

You may find that you grieve for your old identity. The feelings of pain, stress, and tension were all that you've ever known. Your true authentic self is waiting to be discovered! Sometimes we don't even realize that we are in unhealthy circumstances. It's been a part of our life for so long that it has become acceptable and normal. Pain and depression become a lifestyle; it's not just negative feelings. You have the power to break this cycle, and the first step is awareness. If you are not aware of people and circumstances that are not healthy for you, then it can be challenging to make changes and adjustments to relationships.

Note to myself　　　　　Date _____

Just because challenges were part of your past, doesn't mean that it's your destiny. Who or what habit do you need to address in your life in order to start a new healthy chapter in your life?

_____

_____

_____

_____

_____

Day 107

Emotions are an expression, an echo from the pain we experienced in the past. Fears are an expression of complex emotions that cannot be translated by the heart.

Become clear today where your fears are stemming from. Are they real? Are they valid? If you are harboring negative emotions, then explore which unresolved circumstances or interactions from your past are hindering you. Allow the past just to be a story now. Let it be. There is no benefit in keeping an experience from your past alive that only caused you pain because you hold the misery alive.

Note to myself   Date _____

What action can you take today to be more in control of your life and goals?

_____

_____

_____

_____

_____

_____

_____

_____

_____

Day 108

They say, "if it doesn't break you, then it will make you stronger." Well, that would depend on how a person reacts to trauma after surviving it.

Trauma does not necessarily make a person stronger. It can cause a person to be less sensitive to future trauma, which means that they have suppressed and dissociated from their past trauma, only to relive the emotional consequences of their experience in the near future once it has been triggered by their current circumstances. People often think that trauma and challenging times make you stronger; well it doesn't always. It may only desensitize you to your circumstances and events that were painful. In this case, it means that your threshold for experiencing a particular type of emotional pain and stress becomes numb.

Note to myself   Date _____

There are people who go the opposite way, they become even more traumatized by their circumstances and, if their situation is not resolved and dealt with, will suffer psychological consequences. Explore your level of sensitivity to stressful circumstances and how your respond to them. Do you run? Do you want to hide? Do you want to fight? Do you overact, or perhaps not react at all? When you have your answer, back track this type of response. I often find what works best is if I meditate for 5 minutes and ask my unconscious mind to show me, or give me a feeling when this pattern started. Take the leap, heal and resolve this.

Day 109

We have often found ourselves in a place where we are lost because our leaders are blind. They are blind to the needs of humanity.

In hindsight, we don't need leadership, especially leadership whose eyes are wide shut. You know what your journey requires from you, keep moving forward and see that you are exactly where you need to be.

Note to myself   Date _____

In which aspect of your life have you given too much power away to outside influences? What action can you take today to bring more balance?

_____

_____

_____

_____

_____

_____

_____

_____

_____

_____

_____

Day 110

Healing work does not have to conflict with one's religion. It is a resource or tool that is similar to visiting a doctor, dentist, or psychologist.

Healing work can be compared to seeing any professional for help, including a teacher, attorney, or doctor. All these people can help someone without religion coming into it. Don't allow old values or family beliefs to hold you back from a path that your soul knows it needs to embark on.

Note to myself   Date _____

Which old family values or beliefs are holding you back?

_____

_____

_____

_____

_____

_____

_____

_____

_____

_____

_____

Day 111

Never manifest what you want from a place of need, your manifestations will only be met by more need. Manifest your goals, because deep down you know you deserve it!

When you energize "lack" such as "I don't have enough support," you will find yourself more and more in place of the very thing that you feel you lack. When you energize 'I need,' you will find that you need more.

Note to myself   Date _____

When you manifest, allow that manifestation to come from a place of worthiness. Know that you deserve the very thing that you are searching for. Where in your life do you feel you are unworthy of what you want and why? How can you start to change that today? What do you need to believe in yourself in order to know you can have it?

_____

_____

_____

_____

_____

_____

_____

_____

Day 112

Fear by itself cannot be healed, but it is not an independent emotion.

Fear is a symptom of unresolved trauma. Working on a symptom will only cause the problem to resurface again. Find the source of the fear and heal the cause. Set yourself free once and for all from a fear that has been hindering your happiness and progress in life.

Note to myself   Date _____

Give your biggest fear a voice today. What does it say to you? Take your power back from this fear. What can you do differently to be and feel more empowered?

_____

_____

_____

_____

_____

_____

_____

_____

_____

_____

_____

Day 113

Trauma is just trauma. Your biological make-up holds on to it and gives you the illusion that it is still real and taking place in your life. Allow your spirit to meet your body, so that it can become coherent and decide what is real and what is not. Are you ready for your awakening?

Are you ready to wake up from your coma, a life that has been programmed into your ancestry and present life? A life that is controlled and dominated by expectations. Expectations that have been set to serve another's agenda, yet there is no benefit for you in being a puppet for someone else's game. Haven't you already paid a high enough price by following society?

Note to myself   Date _____

Where does that leave you emotionally, spiritually, and mentally? I am not saying that you should rebel. What I am saying is use your discernment and listen to your intuition. When your gut tells you that something is wrong, then it probably is. Where in your life do you feel you have failed to listen to your intuition? What can you do differently to avoid that mistake again? What did you fail to feel, see, or sense?

_____

_____

_____

_____

_____

_____

Day 114

We all get our information from the same source. It's how you interpret and convey the information that makes you so unique and special.

Yes, you are unique! Just because you don't always feel connected to your gifts and talents (or are even aware of them) doesn't mean that you are not unique! If you weren't unique, then you wouldn't be here. Your presence and your life have a purpose that is so deeply interlinked with everyone else. Together we make a difference, and as individuals, we continue to propel the higher intention of the collective consciousness.

Note to myself   Date _____

What is your strength? This can be art, communication, love, friendship and so forth. How have you failed to appreciate your strengths? Which strength are you going to focus on today?

_____

_____

_____

_____

_____

_____

_____

_____

_____

Day 115

Trauma and stress can create specific changes in inherited factors, such as boundaries and trust, which creates what I call inherited trauma. This inherited trauma forms a false barrier that may cause a person to hold on to the stressful memory, thinking it keeps them safe.

I invite you today to explore where you can see certain patterns from your family line and or parents that you are expressing as well. Explore especially the way that you express your boundaries. How do you express your fears?

Note to myself   Date _____

Are you reacting from your authentic feelings or are you responding to an inherited program or pattern that you observed during your childhood?

_____

_____

_____

_____

_____

_____

_____

_____

Day 116

Be at peace with your past, without anger and regret. Be present and fearless in your life as you move into the future that you asked for.

I invite you to write a short letter to your teenage self. Keep the letter positive! There should be no "don't do this, or you will regret it." Be encouraging, positive. and reassuring. Write down at least five bullet points before listening to the healing meditation.

Note to myself   Date _____

_____

_____

_____

_____

_____

_____

_____

_____

_____

_____

_____

_____

Day 117

Did you know that throughout the majority of your life you might express trauma, emotions, habits, and medical symptoms that didn't necessarily start with you?

Many traumas are related to ancestral trauma. You may also unconsciously express trauma that stemmed from conception, development in the womb or from your parents.

Note to myself   Date _____

Which aspects of your parents' are you expressing? What can you do differently today to honor your own truth and self-expression?

_____

_____

_____

_____

_____

_____

_____

_____

_____

_____

_____

Day 118

A new world is waiting for you! Dance to the song of your soul today, be in alignment with your truth, the only restriction in your life is fear. Walk-in your power today and let the veil of illusions fade. A new world will be waiting for you!

Sometimes we need to let go, let go of the need to control, let of the need always to do it right. Yes, that's right; just let it go. The more control we try to have over a situation, the more challenges we will most likely face. When we energize fear of loss and a deep need to always be in control, then that is what your circumstances will allow you to experience.

Note to myself   Date _____

Find balance today and with discernment just let it go. What can you do differently today to embody this state of mind with discernment?

_____

_____

_____

_____

_____

_____

_____

Day 119

A person can form a negative association with an emotion or experience that was supposed to be positive if this pattern is repeated enough. You can break through the barriers; you are not a victim of your past.

It's like being programmed with incorrect reference points due to trauma or stressful events. It's similar to linking up specific wires in a machine incorrectly. The machine won't necessarily explode; however, it won't work very well either, and you will not get the full use of performance out of it. Our brain is the same way!

Note to myself   Date _____

I invite you today to explore where you might perhaps have a negative association with a positive emotion or feeling. For example, when you think about love and you want love, your heart warms up, yet when you meet that special person who just wants to give you love, you sabotage the relationship. You have a negative association with love, yet consciously you know it should be a positive experience, you run away from it. Let go of old negative associations that no longer serve you.

_____

_____

_____

_____

_____

_____

Day 120

Forgiveness means that you have given up trying to change a past that no longer exits.

He who is devoid of the power to forgive, is devoid of the power to love ~ Marlin Luther King Jr.

Note to myself   Date _____

With whom or what do you not feel at peace with today? If you feel discomfort, then I invite you to ask yourself what do you perhaps unconsciously fail to see that could allow you to be and feel free from an old restriction or person in your life?

_____

_____

_____

_____

_____

_____

_____

_____

_____

_____

_____

Day 121

Did you know? When we survive a stressful event, there is no release of the nervous energy, and we carry the stress and memory of the stress for the rest of our life. According to epigenetic and cellular memory research, this trauma can be passed on to future generations!

You are an expression of your ancestry. It's incredible how our biological make-up defines how we react and interact with our environment and also even defines ourselves.

Note to myself   Date _____

Make a list of positive attributes that you can embody today that will support what you envision for your future.

_____

_____

_____

_____

_____

_____

_____

_____

_____

_____

_____

Day 122

When you address a physical injury, you are working with the actual physical trauma, emotional shock, and the survival instincts that were triggered during the time of the injury.

Did you know that when the body experiences physical pain, it creates a small (depending on the trauma experienced) weakening in the fascia where the injury took place? The weakened area (emotionally or physically) in the fascia holds on to the emotion that was experienced at the time of the injury.

Note to myself   Date _____

This could apply to emotional scars as well. Which old emotional or physical wound do you have that gets triggered often? Have you realized your identity exceeds this experience? What do you need to see differently in your life in order to know that you are so much more than an old memory?

_____

_____

_____

_____

_____

_____

_____

_____

Day 123

Hidden benefits are often the reason why people don't completely heal from their past and current hardships, also known as secondary gain.

Hidden benefits can stop you dead in your tracks from letting go of old habits and patterns. The problem is serving you in some way. Even blaming others for any problems, illness and emotional states that you experience can become a hidden benefit. Blaming versus taking action, finding solutions and being proactive rather than being submissive.

Note to myself   Date _____

Where in your life have you neglected your willpower and drive for happiness?

_____

_____

_____

_____

_____

_____

_____

_____

_____

_____

Day 124

Those who need to micromanage (control) everything in their environment have a great need for safety. Their controlling manner is a means of overcompensating for the lack of control they may have had during their childhood and adolescent years.

Don't let your pain from the past rob you from living a life that is unrestricted and free. The more you understand yourself, and why you behave the way you do, the safer you feel. Those who need to be in control are often very territorial, as this is a way of securing their environment and their feelings within a comfort zone that feels familiar. Identify and resolve the secondary gain of any control drama (resolve the fear).

Note to myself   Date _____

For example, if you need to control everything, pretend you've lost complete control of your life. What fear surfaces when you imagine this? Identify it and gently start working towards resolving the attachment you have to be in control. Being in control of your life and circumstances is healthy however, it should never rob you of your sense of freedom and happiness.

_____

_____

_____

_____

_____

_____

Day 125

Trust is a process of setting healthy boundaries, opening some doors and closing others and knowing that you are making the right decisions. Trust truly sets in when the body has learned to trust the soul.

Trust issues are one of the main control dramas in a person's life. Are you a trusting person or are you an example of once bitten, twice shy? Do others trust you? It's normal in today's society to be distrustful. Trust has been so abused and taken advantage of in so many different ways that people prefer not to trust. By not trusting they are unconsciously setting a boundary. This boundary does not stem from a place of confidence and feeling worthy. It stems from a place of pain and being taken advantage of.

Note to myself   Date _____

Where in your life do you feel taken advantage of? What steps can you take today to bring more balance in your life?

_____

_____

_____

_____

_____

_____

_____

_____

Day 126

Did you know that physical injuries can trigger old physical trauma in your body that the conscious mind has temporarily forgot?

People often hold on to trauma due to their body's inability to naturally complete a trauma cycle after the moment of shock, or when a stressful event is over. Let me give you an example: If an antelope narrowly escapes an attack by a lion, it is probably traumatized. As soon as the antelope is safe, it goes through a process of shaking off the trauma. The shaking off may resemble a physical action and movement that helped the antelope to survive the threat and pending trauma (e.g., running) as if the animal is completing the act of survival. After a few minutes, it has released the trauma, and it runs away, healthy and free from trauma.

Note to myself   Date _____

It starts grazing again as if nothing had happened. This process is called completing trauma. As humans, we have numbed our ability to discharge this autonomic nervous energy. The human physically survives the trauma, however never completes the trauma cycle. Where in your life do you feel emotionally frozen? What do you need to believe in yourself in order to know that you can be free from this state?

_____

_____

_____

_____

Day 127

Our perception, how we see the world and take in information, is greatly influenced by predisposed trauma from our ancestry. Have you ever imagined what your world would look like if you could see a world that was not affected by your DNA lineage?

The possibilities are infinite! Filters that have been blocking your ability to see and take in the love and joy that is in your life can fall away. Can you imagine what it would feel like to fully live in the moment, in the here and now, just as you are present right now reading this sentence?

Note to myself   Date _____

The magic happens in the present moment; you just miss it by waiting for it to take place in the future. What steps can you take to be more present in your daily life?

_____

_____

_____

_____

_____

_____

_____

_____

Day 128

You will have a profound impact and effect on those around you when you feel and stand strong within yourself and your own identity. It automatically inspires and awakens the same level of clarity within someone else.

Allow yourself to shine today; don't undermine your talents and gifts. You can be a 'gift' to someone else by just being you!

Note to myself   Date _____

Which aspect of yourself are you rejecting? How can you love that part of yourself more today and fully accept yourself?

_____

_____

_____

_____

_____

_____

_____

_____

_____

Day 129

Did you know that the more physical pain you are in, the more anger, resentment, sadness, and frustration is being suppressed? Your body is talking, are you listening?

I am not implying that you are an angry or sad person. What I am saying is that there is deep-seated anger that you have buried so deep, the conscious mind is not aware of it any longer. I have learned in practice that the more pain a person is in, the deeper and more intense the anger or sadness is that they are unconsciously holding onto. You see, what I have learned is that anger transforms into tension and tension then turns into rigidity and stiffness. If there is an area in the body that was either injured or has been under strain, then this is the area that is likely to flare up. Pain in the body is like a magnet for anger.

Note to myself   Date _____

What are your true feelings today?

_____

_____

_____

_____

_____

_____

_____

Day 130

People go through different stages in their lives. They create and survive challenging circumstances that push them forward in life until their biological state finally meets their spiritual state of mind.

When your body finally becomes coherent with your spirit, you become more in sync with everyone and everything. By this point, what you once thought you needed and wanted has changed. You begin to understand the difference between what will help you achieve your very best and what will not. It is the difference between knowing what you want versus what you need to reach your full potential.

Note to myself   Date _____

I invite you today to explore where you might perhaps have a negative association with a positive emotion or feeling. For example, when you think about love and you want love, your heart warms up, yet when you meet that special person who wants to give you love, you sabotage the relationship. You have a negative association with love, yet consciously you know it should be a positive experience, you run away from it.

_____

_____

_____

_____

_____

_____

Day 131

Pursuing a goal or person that is not meant for your path will only disappoint your expectations.

Do you know what you want from life? Do you want something because you desperately need it or do you want it because you are worthy and feel deserving of it? These two factors and the intentions that you have when you ask for what you 'think' you want can determine how your goals show up in your life.

Note to myself   Date _____

When you set a goal, make sure your intention for the goal is based on your deepest desire that is ignited by your worth of having this goal come into your life. What do you need to believe in yourself in order to know that you deserve this?

_____

_____

_____

_____

_____

_____

_____

_____

_____

Day 132

Thoughts and organs each have a frequency, tone, or vibration. Past illnesses may have gone away. However, they have not entirely healed. A disease may have gone into remission; however, the vibration and cellular memory of the disease can still be in the body.

This is especially true if you have had a problematic organ removed. The emotional issue that caused the organ to become problematic has not been resolved. Only the physical aspect has been removed. The memory of the problem and tension remains in the area where the organ was. Once you have resolved the emotional conflict related to the physical area of the body, the tension or pain dissipates.

Note to myself   Date _____

This concept is true for emotional pain as well. Write down 3 main pain points that you have in your life. Then write down the opposite positive form of this. What can you start to do differently in your life to embrace the positive points more?

_____

_____

_____

_____

_____

_____

Day 133

The only thing that stops you from creating what you want in your life is a resourceful state of mind and emotion, which is blocked by stressful events from your past.

This is simple and straightforward. It's not easy to be happy when you are angry. It's not easy to be joyful when you feel angry. It's not easy to feel creative and resourceful when you are stressed. I invite you to create more structure in your life, where you can have more time to yourself without guilt. Focus more on what makes you happy. The benefits of being happy will have a positive ripple effect in all areas of your life!

Note to myself   Date _____

What is your definition of happiness?

_____

_____

_____

_____

_____

_____

_____

_____

Day 134

Never pity another person. You undermine their ability to cope with their circumstances; some people need more time to find their way.

Pitying them leaves a trail of disempowerment and unnecessary judgment in their lives. Pity is not a form of love; it's often an inaccurate judgment based on very little information. Shift your perspective. You can, however, extend a hand of support, show kindness and believe in someone else so strongly that they regain their self-believe again!

Note to myself   Date _____

Where in your life have you stopped believing in yourself?

_____

_____

_____

_____

_____

_____

_____

_____

_____

_____

Day 135

Self-sabotage occurs when someone undermines his or her progress, whether consciously or unconsciously.

This has happened to all of us. This happens in almost every aspect of our lives. Our mind wants something, yet our actions do something else. This is a form of escape. Needing to get away from a routine or something that burdens you.!

Note to myself   Date _____

There is a part of you that stopped believing in yourself. I invite you today to find and reconnect to that part of you that is amazing and brilliant. Think back to all the times when you did something right, look back on all your achievements and the things you did that brought joy to others. Reconnect to the satisfaction you had when you accomplished what you had set your mind to. I invite you to rediscover your self-belief today.

_____

_____

_____

_____

_____

_____

_____

_____

Day 136

I don't like the word 'mistake,' I call it experimenting.

We often take life too seriously. We all make mistakes. Some of us beat ourselves up when we make a mistake, however, what is the benefit in that? It's not going to change the outcome or fix the problem. It will only leave you feeling worse and less resourceful! Keep experimenting! We all eventually get it right!

Note to myself   Date _____

Where in your life can you be more playful?

_____

_____

_____

_____

_____

_____

_____

_____

_____

_____

_____

Day 137

My past mistakes resulted in my healing journey, becoming painfully long and unnecessarily hard. Forget about forgiveness; it will come naturally when the time is right. Focus on your future goals and how you would like your life to change. Dream, envision, and take action!

I wasted so much of my time trying to force myself to forgive people whom I was not ready to forgive. Little did I realize that it was because of the anger, powerlessness, and resentment that I felt toward them that I haven't dealt with my pain and resentment.

Note to myself   Date _____

Forgiveness is a natural process; you know when the time is right to take that step. Instead, focus on what is robbing you of your freedom, joy and quality of life. What negative pattern has stopped serving you, yet you are holding on to it for dear life? Which negative thoughts are you entertaining and how are they contributing to your life and day-to-day activities? Today I invite you to dream, envision and take action! What is your intention today?

_____

_____

_____

_____

_____

_____

Day 138

Taking responsibility for yourself and the choices that you've made is empowering! You are not responsible for someone else's behavior. Taking responsibility = taking charge of your future and emotional state.

Taking responsibility for your future is the only way you will heal and make personal progress—no one else can heal for you, and no one else other than yourself can move you forward in your life. It is also a vital step in taking your power back.

Note to myself   Date _____

Where in your life have you given your power away? What steps can you take today to start reclaiming it?

_____

_____

_____

_____

_____

_____

_____

_____

_____

_____

Day 139

Do you want to free up your energy? Then let go of what or who you are trying to become someone else other than your true authentic self. Know that you are exactly where you need to be.

Your life will unfold as it should. If we were meant to be "that person" that you are dreaming of right now, then that is what you would have been. Trust the path that you are following. Something even bigger, brighter, and more fulfilling than what you thought you needed could be waiting for you.

Note to myself   Date _____

Trust, allow, have discernment, understand, have awareness and then let go. Where in your life have you been pressuring yourself too much and why?

_____

_____

_____

_____

_____

_____

_____

_____

Day 140

We often become so stuck in our failures that, funnily enough, we fail to see the opportunities that are passing by us.

The past is not going to get you to where you need to be. You learn, let go and move on to the next opportunity or method. Living in the present moment and a clear intention will lead you to the path of success.

Note to myself   Date _____

What steps can you take today to be more present with yourself and goals?

_____

_____

_____

_____

_____

_____

_____

_____

_____

_____

_____

_____

Day 141

Did you know that when a person resolves secondary gains related to trauma, the body starts to remember how to release stress more easily? It no longer has any secondary benefits holding the old stress in place.

This allows the body to naturally switch the instinctive reactions off, instead of it being "on" or activated all the time.

Note to myself   Date _____

Which old stress and emotion are you holding onto that no longer serves your future path? I invite you to go through the Guided Emotional Healing Session at www.guidedhealingsession.com once you have written it down.

_____

_____

_____

_____

_____

_____

_____

_____

_____

Day 142

People see what they want to see based on what they believe in.

Your perception is your reality.

Note to myself   Date _____

What state of mind do you need to embrace today in order to see the positive circumstances in your life?

_____

_____

_____

_____

_____

_____

_____

_____

_____

_____

_____

_____

_____

_____

Day 143

Willpower is a state of mind, the more you use it, the stronger it becomes until you can live your life from a place of strength and determination.

Willpower and self-belief are what propel us forward in life to achieve our dreams. Do you remember that feeling you had when you finally achieved something that you set your heart on? There are also times when we lose sight of these inner resources that propelled us through challenging times while we were in pursuit of our goals.

Note to myself   Date _____

Remember, you already know what this resourceful state feels like. Find this resource again, you have experienced it before and you know what it feels like. You felt it when you accomplished that one dream or goal that you envisioned. When you feel that you have lost your passion and willpower to move forward in life, think back to a time when your willpower was so strong that no one could sway you from that path. Write down what it felt like. What can you do differently today to ignite the memories of these points?

_____

_____

_____

_____

_____

_____

Day 144

Success has two rules:

#1 Never give up and keep being creative.

#2 Repeat step #1.

We all have setbacks in life, whether it's emotional or in our career. The secret to happiness and success is that you should never let go of the drive and motivation that set you on the path to achieving your goals.

Note to myself   Date _____

Movement and creativity = success and happiness. Where in your life have you become stagnant and why?

_____

_____

_____

_____

_____

_____

_____

_____

_____

_____

_____

Day 145

Did you know that Mirror Neurons help us share information with each other without needing to communicate verbally?

These remarkable little neurons that are on the side of your head (temples) help us to relate to our environment and interact with people. In my latest research, I have found that there might be a big possibility that depression could be related to how well these neurons are interacting.

Note to myself   Date _____

Where in your life do you feel you have disconnected from a loved one? What can you do and embrace today that would allow you to reconnect?

_____

_____

_____

_____

_____

_____

_____

_____

_____

_____

Day 146

Be present be in the here and now. This is where the magic happens!

When you have made a mistake, learn from it, let go and move forward. The faster you recover from a mishap or 'speed bump' in life, the quicker you can get back on track. Shift your awareness to the present and let go of the past; the present moment is so much richer with new possibilities!

Note to myself   Date _____

Give yourself permission to make a mistake and instead of beating yourself up, realize that perhaps a new method is needed. How can you be more playful and creative with your goals today?

_____

_____

_____

_____

_____

_____

_____

_____

_____

Day 147

Your vibe is your handshake before you have even spoken one word.

We are all intuitive and sensitive. Some of us place more focus on these abilities than others. Choose how you want to show up in the world and in the company of others.

Note to myself   Date _____

If you feel blocked in becoming that person, the amazing and radiant person that you truly are, then it's time to backtrack and let go of patterns that no longer serve you. What steps can you take today to allow your strengths to come forward? What do you need to believe in yourself in order to allow this to take place today?

_____

_____

_____

_____

_____

_____

_____

_____

_____

_____

Day 148

Depression is a condition that can turn into a lifestyle.

Note to myself   Date _____

Write down a list of what you will see and hear differently in your life if you fully embraced a peaceful and content state of mind. What small steps can you start to take today to make this your everyday reality?

_____

_____

_____

_____

_____

_____

_____

_____

_____

_____

_____

_____

_____

_____

Day 149

The only thing that stops you from creating what you want in your life is a resourceful state of mind.

You are an expression of your ancestry, and your ancestry has accumulated many resourceful states, which are recorded and held in your biological make-up. The good news? Those resourceful memories are part of your biological make-up.

Note to myself   Date _____

Where in your life do you feel un-resourceful? What do you need to believe in yourself in order to know that you have what it takes to become fully resourceful again?

_____

_____

_____

_____

_____

_____

_____

_____

_____

_____

_____

Day 150

You underestimate your ability to cope in life until the time comes when you have no other choice.

We often only realize how strong we are when we are faced with challenges. We all have inner resources that can help us through dire circumstances. The difference in those who make it is that they are the ones who kept on believing in themselves.

Note to myself   Date _____

Where in your life are you undermining yourself? What can you do differently to restore your confidence within yourself today?

_____

_____

_____

_____

_____

_____

_____

_____

_____

_____

Day 151

Openness and receptivity enhance the process of transformation in your life.

It allows for the most excellent flexibility and impact, which you can have not only in your life but in the lives of others. You are a walking channel of wisdom and infinity.

Note to myself   Date _____

What small action can you take today to bring a positive influence and impact on someone else's life today?

_____

_____

_____

_____

_____

_____

_____

_____

_____

_____

_____

_____

Day 152

There is already a predisposition within you that allows you to experience a variety of emotions and resources! You are a powerful resourceful being. Stop underestimating yourself.

Traits/emotions/patterns you are born with may surface in your life from a very young age, as you begin to interact with the world. Be the driver of your growth. Ultimately you determine the quality of life that you experience. You don't have to be rich to feel abundant. You don't have to be on a beach to feel free.

Note to myself   Date _____

Where in your life do you feel stuck? What mindset can you embrace today to mentally set yourself free?

_____

_____

_____

_____

_____

_____

_____

_____

_____

Day 153

Dance to the rhythm of your soul.

We are all responsible for our future and how we choose to live our lives. It is our responsibility to decide how we are going to move forward from our past every day.

Note to myself   Date _____

What can you let go of today that no longer serves your future and pursuit for happiness?

_____

_____

_____

_____

_____

_____

_____

_____

_____

_____

_____

_____

_____

Day 154

Love is supposed to flow. If you can't let it flow, then let it go.

When you try to manipulate and control love, or how someone feels about you, then you might find yourself in circumstances that are not for your highest and best. What is your definition of love? Are your values for love being respected? How do you allow others to love you? Are you able to love yourself? What will it take for you to break down the barriers that are sabotaging true and healthy love from flowing into your life?

Your task is not to seek for love, but merely to seek and find all the barriers within yourself that you have built against it ~ Rumi

Note to myself   Date _____

What is your definition of love? When you look at the answer, ask yourself, 'how am I not giving that to myself?'

_____

_____

_____

_____

_____

_____

_____

_____

Day 155

When you take responsibility for your healing journey and future, you are taking control of your life and emotions. Your life is not controlled and dominated by your past.

Is there a state of mind that is more powerful than this?

Note to myself   Date _____

Which old memory is hindering you from moving forward in your life? What in your life will change that you might not be ready to change if you did let go of this old memory?

_____

_____

_____

_____

_____

_____

_____

_____

_____

_____

_____

_____

_____

Day 156

The more you are de-attached to a specific outcome; the less you can be intimidated.

Today is all about letting go of unhealthy attachment.

Note to myself   Date _____

Where in your life have you been holding onto unhealthy people or circumstances that no longer support your emotional and spiritual growth? What steps can you take today to strengthen your relationship with yourself that would ultimately allow you to rely less on old outdated relationships?

_____

_____

_____

_____

_____

_____

_____

_____

_____

_____

_____

Day 157

Forgiveness is to understand your actions and reactions to the behaviors of others or circumstances. It does not mean you have to accept what has happened.

Note to myself   Date _____

In which aspect of your own life do you perhaps need to forgive yourself?

_____

_____

_____

_____

_____

_____

_____

_____

_____

_____

_____

_____

_____

_____

Day 158

You are the answer and solution to your problems.

The answer and solution will find you, or you might even find it, by just being open and receptive to new methods and options. Let go of rigidity and go with the flow!

Note to myself   Date _____

Where in your life can you be more playful and in the flow?

_____

_____

_____

_____

_____

_____

_____

_____

_____

_____

_____

_____

_____

_____

_____

Day 159

Has your pain and history become your identity? Maybe it's time to reclaim your true authentic self!

Your physical, emotional pain, and past is not your identity! It's an experiences that influenced you.

Note to myself   Date _____

Now, create new experiences that can influence you in a positive way and start writing a history that will only make you smile.

_____

_____

_____

_____

_____

_____

_____

_____

_____

_____

_____

_____

_____

Day 160

"People are like tides and waves of the ocean. Some are gentle, and some are destructive, however, they never stay on the beach. They always move away, change, and never come back in the same shape, way or form." Make allowances for positive change, because, without flexibility, we will cease to exist.

Note to myself   Date _____

Where in your life can you be more flexible?

_____

_____

_____

_____

_____

_____

_____

_____

_____

_____

_____

_____

Day 161

You can't change the laws of nature, and you can't change the past.

What you can change is how you perceive events. You can change how you are going to move forward from them and how they affect you right now.

The power of change lies within you.

Note to myself   Date _____

Where in your life do you feel held back? What can you do differently today that will allow you to set yourself emotionally free from these circumstances or relationships?

_____

_____

_____

_____

_____

_____

_____

_____

_____

_____

Day 162

You are the force behind the force, and you are the law behind the law; it's never outside of yourself.

The only thing that sets us apart from one another is our experiences, body, and genetic make-up. People's feelings of lack of worthiness often hold them back and block them from realizing that they can be the creator of their life right now.

Note to myself   Date _____

What are you lacking the most in your life today? What steps can you take today to fulfill the void that you feel and realize that you are worthy of what you want and need?

_____

_____

_____

_____

_____

_____

_____

_____

_____

_____

_____

Day 163

Where does your power lie? People who look outside of themselves for answers and guidance are not ready to step into their full glory and power.

Are you ready?

Note to myself   Date _____

What in your life will change that you are not ready to change if you did fully step into your power today?

_____

_____

_____

_____

_____

_____

_____

_____

_____

_____

_____

_____

_____

Day 164

If we have this amazing source of consciousness and wisdom within, why do people insist on seeing their inspiration as something that comes from "upstairs" or outside of themselves?

That source of consciousness and wisdom is within you. We are not separate, from one another, our thought pattern is just flawed by an ego that wants to dominate and be unique.

Note to myself   Date _____

What can you embrace more of in your life that will nurture and bring forth your uniqueness and gifts to the world?

_____

_____

_____

_____

_____

_____

_____

_____

_____

_____

_____

Day 165

Begin your day with a new and positive attitude and not with the pain from yesterday.

Pain can often push you to move forward and to make changes, but why wait for the pain to set in before taking action?

Note to myself   Date _____

Emotional or physical discomfort is a call to action. Where in your life do you need to take action to bring balance back?

_____

_____

_____

_____

_____

_____

_____

_____

_____

_____

_____

_____

_____

Day 166

Have you realized how resourceful you suddenly become when you have a super urgent issue to resolve? When there is no pressure, you often feel blocked and that you lack creativity?

Learn to become resourceful without needing stress to motivate you. Learn to trust yourself and know that you always know exactly what to do!

Note to myself   Date _____

_____

_____

_____

_____

_____

_____

_____

_____

_____

_____

_____

_____

Day 167

Many spiritual and in-depth experiences occur when you are unable to accept your divinity.

Our self-worth often makes us feel that it's easier to believe that you are speaking to God rather than to think that God is within.

Note to myself   Date _____

How can you embrace and nurture your spirituality today?

_____

_____

_____

_____

_____

_____

_____

_____

_____

_____

_____

_____

_____

_____

Day 168

I am grateful for all that I have, all that I am and all that I have achieved!

_____

Note to myself   Date _____

Your home-play for today is to answer these questions. The trick is that your answer has to be positive! What are you grateful for today? Who loves you? Who do you love? What are excited about today?

_____

_____

_____

_____

_____

_____

_____

_____

_____

_____

_____

_____

_____

_____

Day 169

Negative emotions do not necessarily require a conscious effort for it to be experienced or communicated. They are merely a symptom of unresolved stress.

Your emotions are not always related to conscious thought and effort. When the unconscious mind comes into the equation, that is when things can become complicated, yet you are not a victim of your thoughts.

Note to myself   Date _____

Give your negative thoughts a voice today. What is the deep underlying message of it? What positive action can you take today to ease old negative thoughts that no longer serve you?

_____

_____

_____

_____

_____

_____

_____

_____

_____

_____

Day 170

The next choice that you make can change your life. Your choices reflect who you become. If you want to live a better experience, then make better choices with more awareness and by being patient with the process that is unfolding. If you are going to be a person, then make better choices.

It all starts with the next choice that you make.

Note to myself   Date _____

Where in your life can you practice more patience with yourself when you are faced with a challenged?

_____

_____

_____

_____

_____

_____

_____

_____

_____

_____

_____

Day 171

Often when a person changes, it is not always a change for the better. The façade became too much of a burden to carry.

When you are not authentic and truthful, baggage can become burdensome, weigh you down and ultimately rob you of your quality of life. Be true to yourself, and if you see that people in your life are not true to themselves or you, then remember this one thing, always stay true to yourself.

Note to myself   Date _____

Do you have a fear of being your true authentic self? What do you need to believe in yourself in order to know that who you are is enough and good enough?

_____

_____

_____

_____

_____

_____

_____

_____

_____

_____

Day 172

Don't judge me for who I am, you have not seen my past and you have not seen my victories.

"Judge a man by his questions rather than his answers" ~ Voltaire

Note to myself   Date _____

Which aspect of your past are you grateful for? What about your future are you excited about?

_____

_____

_____

_____

_____

_____

_____

_____

_____

_____

_____

_____

_____

Day 173

The greatest things in life are often the things that cannot be seen.

"This is love: to fly toward a secret sky, to cause a hundred veils to fall each moment. First to let go of life. Finally, to take a step without feet." ~ Rumi

Note to myself   Date _____

This is especially true for emotions. Which emotional state will bring you closer to your loved ones today?

_____

_____

_____

_____

_____

_____

_____

_____

_____

_____

_____

_____

_____

Day 174

Don't try to explain who you are, just be it!

You don't need anyone's permission to be your authentic self.

Note to myself   Date _____

What action can you take to embrace your authentic identity today?

_____

_____

_____

_____

_____

_____

_____

_____

_____

_____

_____

_____

_____

_____

Day 175

Love and appreciate the people you have in your life. Remember those who made you happy and made you feel loved. Those are the things that cannot be seen, yet these experiences can change your life.

"Everyone has been made for some particular work, and the desire for that work has been put in every heart." ~ Rumi

Note to myself   Date _____

When was the last time you said to yourself 'I love you?' What can you do today that will nurture your relationship with yourself?

_____

_____

_____

_____

_____

_____

_____

_____

_____

_____

Day 176

Emotions may arise in response to changes in your life or environment. Negative emotions are a symptom of deep-seated problems and not the original cause.

Emotions are an expression of genetic programming and your life experiences. You also have positive emotional resources in your genetic make-up. Use them wisely.

"You know the value of every article of merchandise, but if you don't know the value of your own soul, it's all foolishness."

~ Rumi

Note to myself   Date _____

What is your greatest strength? Have any of your recent actions demonstrated this strength?

_____

_____

_____

_____

_____

_____

_____

_____

_____

Day 177

The universe created a plan of action to move you into this exact time and place. Now is your time to share your talents, gifts, and step into your full potential! What are you waiting for?

"Sunlight fell upon the wall; the wall received a borrowed splendor. Why set your heart on a piece of earth, O simple one? Seek out the source which shines forever." ~ Rumi

Note to myself   Date _____

Do you find yourself influencing your world, or it influencing you? What steps can you take today to be and feel more in control of your life?

_____
_____
_____
_____
_____
_____
_____
_____
_____
_____
_____
_____

Day 178

Anger, the time has come, I am breaking up with you, I have fallen in love with happiness.

You will never find happiness and inner peace when you are always in an angry state. Love yourself enough to know that you are worthy, safe, and deserving of living a peaceful life.

Note to myself   Date _____

How does that anger serve you? What will you not achieve in life, if you let go of the anger? Hint, anger is often related to overcorrected boundaries.

_____

_____

_____

_____

_____

_____

_____

_____

_____

_____

_____

_____

_____

Day 179

Don't take people for granted who contribute to your journey, which allowed you to become the best version of you!

Often there are times when we need a helping hand to grow, never forget those who helped you without expecting anything in return. They are called earth angels. Cherish them.

Note to myself   Date _____

Where in your life have you taken your self-worth for granted?

_____

_____

_____

_____

_____

_____

_____

_____

_____

_____

_____

Day 180

Steps to become more powerful in your life:

Build a relationship with yourself. *You have to build a relationship with yourself and stop hating and resenting your failures. How can you form a relationship with yourself if you don't like yourself? You are the one that is spending the most time with yourself. You are the driver.*

Make peace with yourself. *You can start doing this by respecting your boundaries. The moment you become your best friend; you will have a powerful partner in life.*

Note to myself   Date _____

Define what your values are in terms of your relationships, love, friendships Do you know what you want in life? Is what you want in conflict with your values?

Let go of the fear of rejection. You can't live your life fearing rejection; you will not achieve anything! It sabotages your quality of life, relationships, and friendships. How long do you want to live in fear? You are good enough as you are!

Communicate. You can only do this when you know what your values and needs are.

What else can you add to this list?

_____

_____

_____

Day 181

We don't always keep in contact with the people who played the most significant roles in our self-development.

Make sure that you take the time to acknowledge the people who loved you while you made your mistakes, who wiped your tears when no one else was around and who gave you sound advice when you needed it most.

Note to myself   Date _____

Never leave room for regret! Every moment spent in regret is a moment that you could have spent in love and gratitude.

Call someone today who made a positive lasting impact on your life.

_____

_____

_____

_____

_____

_____

_____

_____

_____

_____

Day 182

How are you going to represent yourself today? Just as you take a shower before engaging with the world, meditate and gain clarity in your mind before showing up in the world.

How are you going to show up today?

Note to myself   Date _____

What lasting impression do you want to leave people with today?

_____

_____

_____

_____

_____

_____

_____

_____

_____

_____

_____

_____

_____

Day 183

If a person was born depressed, it does not mean that they were born without the ability to feel happiness and joy. There is merely a biological imbalance that is blocking their mind from experiencing pleasure and bliss. The resources and predisposition are within you!

Happiness is a state of mind; it cannot be searched for; it's not hiding somewhere outside of yourself. It lives within you, and it's waiting for you to rediscover it.

Note to myself   Date _____

What can you do today that will bring more happiness into your life?

_____

_____

_____

_____

_____

_____

_____

_____

_____

_____

Day 184

Acceptance does not equal failure.

When you start to process and untangle negative associations and experiences related to acceptance, the process of accepting becomes easier. Acceptance will no longer be associated with failure, humiliation, or a feeling that you had to cave into something that you may have been fighting against your entire life. You can accept your circumstances or changes that are taking place with more ease, grace, and the feeling of control and even empowerment. You can start to observe your reality with a deeper level of awareness, instead of seeing things from a contaminated perspective. You will have more energy and willingness to focus and to take in that which you need to learn from your life experiences to move on. Instead of blocking your experiences and teachings in life or relationships, you can accept them, learn from them, and move on with no regret.

Note to myself   Date _____

Where in your life could you have mistaken acceptance with failure?

_____

_____

_____

_____

_____

_____

Day 185

Don't give power to your past; it will only sabotage your future.

Your ability to feel joy can be reawakened by clearing away the memories and blocks that suppressed it.

Note to myself   Date _____

Where in your life can you be more playful and joyful?

_____

_____

_____

_____

_____

_____

_____

_____

_____

_____

_____

_____

_____

Day 186

Emotions are a symptom of the original problem and not the problem itself.

We often stay stuck in our lives as we try to resolve a symptom and not the circumstances and how those circumstances made us feel.

Note to myself   Date _____

What is your most dominant negative emotion today? What is the opposite flip side of this emotion? What can you do differently today to allow this positive emotion to surface?

_____
_____
_____
_____
_____
_____
_____
_____
_____
_____
_____
_____

Day 187

Acceptance does not mean that you are weak or have poor boundaries.

Acceptance means that you understand what is going on in your life. You find that more profound meaning, why things are the way that they are. Acceptance is similar to surrendering. Surrendering is by no means giving in to anyone or anything. Surrendering means that you have mastered a level of awareness that allows you to see what is worth your while and what is not and to let go of any unhealthy investment you had in your past circumstances or relationships.

Note to myself   Date _____

Where in your life are you fighting for something that have ceased to serve you?

_____

_____

_____

_____

_____

_____

_____

_____

_____

Day 188

The moment you become your best friend, you will have a powerful lifelong partner who will never let you down. You got this.

No one knows you better than you do.

Note to myself   Date _____

What steps can you take today to improve your relationship with yourself?

_____

_____

_____

_____

_____

_____

_____

_____

_____

_____

_____

_____

_____

Day 189

Resentment prevents you from being in the present, it stops you from falling in love, and it stops you from appreciating all the good things that you have in your life. At some point in the future, you may find that your resentment has been replaced by regret.

Holding onto resentment is a short-term coping mechanism that can become emotionally destructive. It's a high price to pay for it robs you of your joy and quality of life.

Note to myself   Date _____

In which area of your life has resentment become dominant? What do you need to believe in yourself in order to know that you no longer need to hold onto resentment?

_____

_____

_____

_____

_____

_____

_____

_____

_____

_____

Day 190

Give people enough love, guidance, and support to allow them to make the best decision and choices for their future.

Negative thoughts, emotional patterns, and values can be projected onto another. As a result, if they are repeated on a regular basis, one day, those patterns can become a person's absolute truth and foundation.

Note to myself   Date _____

Have you been the kind of friend you would want as one?

_____

_____

_____

_____

_____

_____

_____

_____

_____

_____

_____

_____

Day 191

To dwell in a state of 'aloneness' means you have accepted that you are unlovable and not good enough. You are so much more than that. Stop enabling people's opinions of you that are based on their false and flawed perception. Their truth is not your truth.

You are enough. You are good enough as you are. You were born in God's image; you are a beacon of love and light.

Note to myself   Date _____

Where in your life have you undermined and ignored your own truth?

_____

_____

_____

_____

_____

_____

_____

_____

_____

_____

_____

Day 192

It is important to learn to love again and to trust in love. You can only do that by learning to trust yourself before trusting in others. Not everyone in life will leave you. Some people who will see your value and beauty.

Those who suffered from abandonment often surround themselves with unhealthy people and unhealthy relationships to fill a bottomless empty void with more poison.

Note to myself   Date _____

I invite you today to explore what your definition of love and relationships are. How you were made to feel about yourself and your needs are often reflected in the relationships you attract in life. The people in your life might actually be the best teachers, to show you what you need to change within yourself in order to live the life that you deserve.

_____

_____

_____

_____

_____

_____

_____

_____

Day 193

Anger and rage are not actual emotions. They are a reaction to deep unresolved pain and overstepped boundaries.

Note to myself   Date _____

Where in your life has anger become your boundary and defensive mechanism? What steps can you take today to bring more balance in your emotional life?

_____

_____

_____

_____

_____

_____

_____

_____

_____

_____

_____

_____

_____

_____

Day 194

Anger does not equal confidence. It creates a false sense of empowerment that is driven by fear.

People often use anger to establish boundaries and to manipulate and control.

It's an overcompensation for loss of control and feeling powerless in one's life.

People often feel more confident to express their boundaries when they are upset.

Anger is often used to reclaim one's power and to set boundaries in an unhealthy way.

This could ultimately burn bridges and leave you on your own island.

Note to myself   Date _____

I invite you to make the following acknowledgments and then explore more associations that you have made with anger.

I acknowledge the difference between anger and power.

I acknowledge the difference between anger and confidence.

I acknowledge the difference between anger and

_____

I acknowledge the difference between anger and

_____

Day 195

Anxiety could be your body's way of telling you that new doors and higher levels of consciousness are unveiling themselves. Are you ready for the shift?

Fear of change is common. But what could go wrong if you finally became the best

of you?

Note to myself   Date _____

In which aspect of your life has anxiety taken over? Take five minutes today and give your anxiety a voice. What is it trying to tell you?

_____

_____

_____

_____

_____

_____

_____

_____

_____

_____

_____

Day 196

Don't punish yourself with isolation. Isolation is a much higher price to pay than learning to trust again.

There is a difference between being alone and feeling lonely. Being alone is often a choice and one that is made with contentment. Loneliness is when you realize that you miss the people that you love and can relate to.

Note to myself   Date _____

In which area of your life have you isolated and insulated yourself from? What is the benefit of isolating yourself? Look at the answer to the last question. How can you give that to yourself today without needing to isolate yourself?

_____

_____

_____

_____

_____

_____

_____

_____

_____

_____

Day 197

We are continuously forming and reforming our boundaries based on our life experiences and the sensory messages associated with those encounters.

Positive ongoing experiences reinforce healthy boundaries! Choose your friends and company wisely. Invite people into your life who will bring out the best in you.

Note to myself   Date _____

How easy is it for you to say no? Do you know how to recognize your boundaries? What do you need to believe in yourself in order to know and feel safe, confident and safe to say no when you need to establish a boundary?

_____

_____

_____

_____

_____

_____

_____

_____

_____

Day 198

Power changes people. Many people who seek power stop thinking empathically, they become servers of the material world and neglect their inner world.

Remember who you are at a core level, that part of you never changes. Your ego changes, and that can ultimately transform into someone that not even you can love. Stay true to who you are, show kindness, and be humble.

Note to myself   Date _____

What steps can you take to show more kindness to yourself today?

_____

_____

_____

_____

_____

_____

_____

_____

_____

_____

_____

Day 199

Awareness is the key and first step to self-healing and improving your quality of life.

The better you understand your behavior, actions, and reactions, the more equipped you are for the future that awaits you. Understanding and awareness are tools of clarity that can enable you to move forward fearlessly. It cannot be taken away from you.

Note to myself   Date _____

At what time in your recent past, have you felt most passionate and alive? Think back to the mindset that you energized and how you felt. What can you do differently today to re-awaken your deepest passion?

_____

_____

_____

_____

_____

_____

_____

_____

_____

_____

_____

Day 200

Personal progress requires the kind of acceptance that makes you feel empowered instead of defeated.

Learn to become your cheerleader, never rely on another's feedback or encouragement to be amazing.

Note to myself   Date _____

Make a list of positive affirmations that you can embody today:

I am good enough

I am successful

.... now over to you:

_____

_____

_____

_____

_____

_____

_____

_____

_____

_____

_____

_____

Day 201

Is your need to be in control of everything controlling you?

Pretend that your ability to always be in control is taken away. Who are you now? What is your identity? What is the worst thing that can happen if you just let go?

Note to myself   Date _____

It is important to identify the fear's origin and the reason why it's still there. Write down your fears. What is truly the worst thing that could happen if you trusted your ability to remain in control without having to take action to be in control?

_____

_____

_____

_____

_____

_____

_____

_____

_____

_____

_____

_____

Day 202

Never sacrifice

#1 Your values
#2 Your needs
#3 Your heart
#4 Your dignity

Love yourself enough to have clear and loving boundaries.
Know where your limits are and to respect yourself enough
to exercise and express them.

Note to myself   Date _____

Where in your life have you sacrificed too much of your values
and boundaries? What can you do differently today to bring
more balance into your life?

_____

_____

_____

_____

_____

_____

_____

_____

_____

_____

Day 203

5 Important Steps to Change

#1 Make a decision! Be clear about what you want.

#2 Commit. The moment you commit yourself to your goals, you have a way forward.

#3 Focus on what you want.

 # 4 Act! Nothing is going to happen if you don't take action! Your goal will only end up on your "Wish List."

#5 Create a positive and supportive environment and nurture healthy relationships that can complement your new journey!

Note to myself   Date _____

Look at the people around you and evaluate your circumstances. Are they for your highest and best outcome? Remember, it takes team work to make a dream work. Surround yourself with those who want to see you succeed! Be your own cheerleader. Focus on constructive advice and disregard the rest. Never stop believing in yourself.

_____

_____

_____

_____

_____

_____

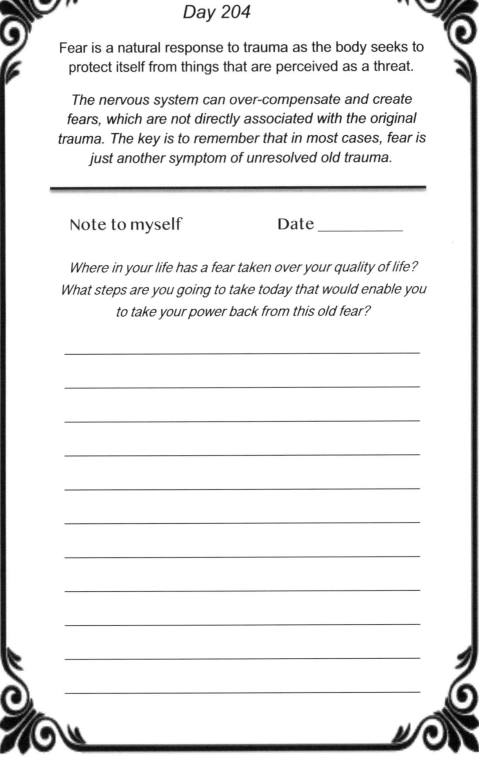

Day 204

Fear is a natural response to trauma as the body seeks to protect itself from things that are perceived as a threat.

The nervous system can over-compensate and create fears, which are not directly associated with the original trauma. The key is to remember that in most cases, fear is just another symptom of unresolved old trauma.

Note to myself   Date _____

Where in your life has a fear taken over your quality of life? What steps are you going to take today that would enable you to take your power back from this old fear?

_____

_____

_____

_____

_____

_____

_____

_____

_____

_____

_____

Day 205

Guilt can set in when you were made to feel that you are wrong for wanting something that your heart longed for.

Guilt is also often a result of being manipulated to adjust to someone else's values while yours were disrespected. This problem starts when boundaries are not expressed, and the manipulation is accepted due to a deep need to be accepted and loved.

Note to myself   Date _____

In which aspect of your life have you sacrificed your values for the sake of being accepted?

_____

_____

_____

_____

_____

_____

_____

_____

_____

_____

_____

Day 206

I used to worry what people thought about me and if they liked me. But things have changed, I have changed. Now I wonder if I like them.

Surround yourself with people who you resonate with. Invite relationships and friendships into your life that bring out the best in you. As you heal and change, so does your environment and relationships.

Note to myself   Date _____

What would make you feel more worthy? What do you believe needs to be different about you? Who made you feel that you had to be this way? I invite you today to take your power back from that person or situation.

_____

_____

_____

_____

_____

_____

_____

_____

_____

_____

Day 207

Pain is an experience. When a person cannot stop or control something in their life, they adapt to the experience. This is the body's way of coping with stress. In most cases, pain can become a part of one's identity. It could ultimately change how you express your authentic self. I have to ask, "Who would you be without your pain?".

You are so much bigger and more powerful than a past that does not exist anymore.

Note to myself   Date _____

Who and what would you be without your pain? Are you holding on to it to stay small and to hide? Invite yourself today to be more playful and carefree with discernment.

_____

_____

_____

_____

_____

_____

_____

_____

_____

_____

Day 208

Never lose your sense of self, trying to hold onto something or someone that no longer serves your purpose.

If these circumstances or a person we're meant to stay, then they will. When you feel rejected, you think you lack support or cannot accomplish your goals on your own. It's human nature to be a part of a community, to work together, live together, and socialize together. At the same time, it is also important to stay true to your unique character, values and needs.

Note to myself   Date _____

Which aspect of yourself have you neglected in order to be part of a community, group of friends or family? What steps can you take today to start reclaiming those aspects of yourself, within yourself?

_____

_____

_____

_____

_____

_____

_____

_____

_____

Day 209

Resentment often serves a purpose, as you can draw personal power from it when it's used to express boundaries and build walls. Being resentful is a high price to pay as it robs you of your joy, identity, and quality of life.

This comes into play when a person is struggling to let go of the actions of people or circumstances that caused them harm or stress.

Note to myself   Date _____

I invite you to ask yourself "How does it benefit me to hold on to memories and relationships that caused me harm or stress? What do I need to believe in myself in order to know that I no longer need this resentment in my life and mind?"

_____

_____

_____

_____

_____

_____

_____

_____

_____

_____

Day 210

I invite you to realize that as of right now, you are in control of your life. This includes your emotional state and your future. How are you going to move forward with this information?

"Yesterday I was clever, so I wanted to change the world. Today I am wise so I am changing myself." ~ Rumi

---

Note to myself   Date _____

Become aware of how you have changed and why? Where in your life have you changed and become someone that was not honoring your true authentic self?

_____

_____

_____

_____

_____

_____

_____

_____

_____

_____

_____

_____

Day 211

The human body has a way of sending messages when you are disconnected from what's going on in your life.

If you are stubborn in your relationship with the truth, if you are rigid, then this will surface strongly in your body. The muscles that hold this stress, as muscles give people both strength and flexibility, they will keep the stress of being inflexible or rigid. The message is clear, listen to your body; it's here to serve you.

Note to myself   Date _____

Have you failed to recently listen to your body and messages it was trying to send you? Revisit this moment and give the stress or pain a voice. If it could speak, what would it say?

_____

_____

_____

_____

_____

_____

_____

_____

_____

_____

Day 212

Showing emotion and kindness is it what makes you human.

People have been brainwashed that they have to be strong, especially men. People have been always to keep it together. Inevitably, people become rigid in their lives as a way of protecting their fragile emotional state. Showing emotions are seen as a weakness. I believe emotions are shown because a person cares about something, be it a value, belief, person, or goal. Passion is expressed through our emotions and actions.

Note to myself   Date _____

Make sure today that your emotions and actions are coherent, it's a recipe for success in your communications, relationships and most importantly of all, your relationship with yourself.

_____

_____

_____

_____

_____

_____

_____

_____

Day 213

Selfishness is driven by lack.

"If you could leave your selfishness, you would see how you've been torturing your soul." ~ Rumi

Note to myself   Date _____

What is your greatest lack in your life? What is stopping you from manifesting your desires? How to find the answer? What in your life will change that you are not ready to change if you did receive what you desired?

_____

_____

_____

_____

_____

_____

_____

_____

_____

_____

_____

_____

Day 214

There is nothing wrong with having an ego – it is often a necessary illusion.

Without an ego, a person would not achieve or aspire to their goals within a competitive environment. It is how this person goes about achieving their success that defines whether the ego is being used in a constructive or destructive way. Your ego is part of your biological make-up, but it doesn't have to control you.

Note to myself   Date _____

In which aspect of your life can you practice being more humble?

_____

_____

_____

_____

_____

_____

_____

_____

_____

_____

_____

Day 215

You don't have to be a victim of your past failures.

Note to myself   Date _____

Where in your life have you given up on a goal because you failed? What do you need to believe in yourself in order to know that you can succeed despite temporary failure?

_____

_____

_____

_____

_____

_____

_____

_____

_____

_____

_____

_____

_____

_____

Day 216

Trust is a process of setting healthy boundaries, opening some doors and closing others, and knowing that you are making the right decisions.

Note to myself   Date _____

What steps can you take today to reinforce your relationship and trust within yourself?

_____

_____

_____

_____

_____

_____

_____

_____

_____

_____

_____

_____

_____

_____

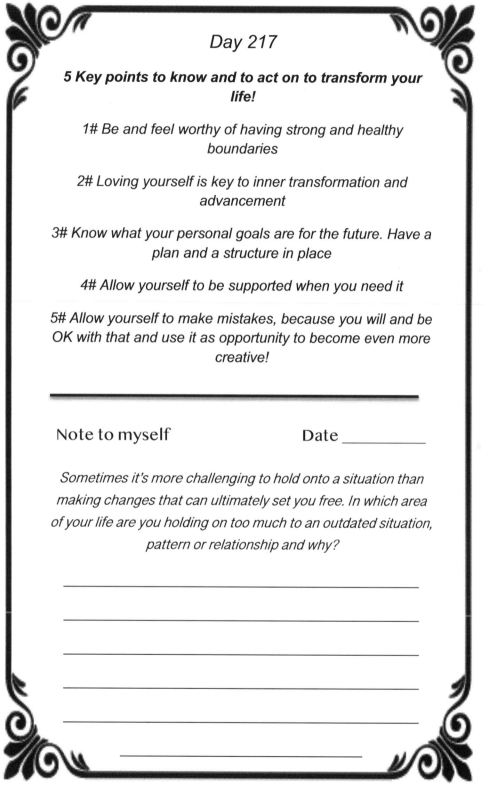

Day 217

5 Key points to know and to act on to transform your life!

1# Be and feel worthy of having strong and healthy boundaries

2# Loving yourself is key to inner transformation and advancement

3# Know what your personal goals are for the future. Have a plan and a structure in place

4# Allow yourself to be supported when you need it

5# Allow yourself to make mistakes, because you will and be OK with that and use it as opportunity to become even more creative!

Note to myself   Date _____

Sometimes it's more challenging to hold onto a situation than making changes that can ultimately set you free. In which area of your life are you holding on too much to an outdated situation, pattern or relationship and why?

_____

_____

_____

_____

_____

_____

Day 218

It is not your task to just give love; it is your mission to discover the blocks that stop you from loving yourself as much as you love others.

Note to myself   Date _____

What can you do for yourself today to reinforce your relationship and self-love within yourself?

_____

_____

_____

_____

_____

_____

_____

_____

_____

_____

_____

_____

_____

_____

_____

Day 219

Learning to trust again, will lead you to new beginnings!

The benefit of dealing with trust issues is that you can begin to feel safe again, reconnect with yourself and sharpen your intuition.

Note to myself   Date _____

In order for you to trust another, you need to trust yourself first. Can you trust yourself today? If the answer is negative, then write down why?

_____

_____

_____

_____

_____

_____

_____

_____

_____

_____

_____

_____

_____

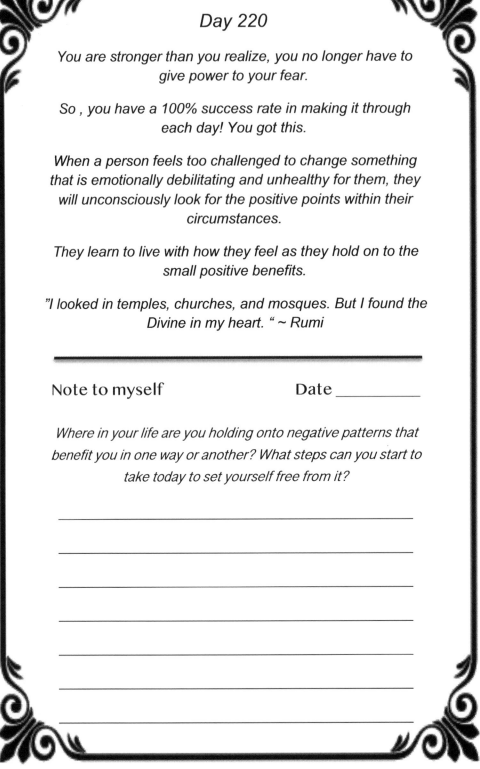

Day 220

You are stronger than you realize, you no longer have to give power to your fear.

So , you have a 100% success rate in making it through each day! You got this.

When a person feels too challenged to change something that is emotionally debilitating and unhealthy for them, they will unconsciously look for the positive points within their circumstances.

They learn to live with how they feel as they hold on to the small positive benefits.

"I looked in temples, churches, and mosques. But I found the Divine in my heart. " ~ Rumi

Note to myself   Date _____

Where in your life are you holding onto negative patterns that benefit you in one way or another? What steps can you start to take today to set yourself free from it?

_____

_____

_____

_____

_____

_____

_____

Day 221

You can't see the shadows when you keep looking at the light.

I invite you today to see the good in people. See the positive opportunities within challenging circumstances.

Note to myself   Date _____

I invite you today to see the good in yourself. Make a list of five qualities that you love about yourself.

_____

_____

_____

_____

_____

_____

_____

_____

_____

_____

_____

_____

Day 222

Every challenge is a test of your faith.

No one can knock you down when you believe in yourself and have faith in your path, even though you might not always see the bigger picture.

"Never lose hope, my dear heart, miracles dwell in the invisible." ~ Rumi

---

Note to myself   Date _____

What steps can you take to restore your faith in yourself today?

_____

_____

_____

_____

_____

_____

_____

_____

_____

_____

_____

_____

Day 223

Be kind to others in your life; we don't always know the journey that they had to endure to get to where they are today.

Note to myself   Date _____

What can you do differently today to show kindness to another and yourself?

_____

_____

_____

_____

_____

_____

_____

_____

_____

_____

_____

_____

_____

_____

Day 224

Blaming others for your problems, illness or emotional state can become a hidden benefit, yes people significantly contributed to them.

Only you can change how they affect you in the future. How pain is expressed can be constructive or destructive. Be creative and never stop moving forward.

You are the driver who is driving you to your destiny.

Note to myself   Date _____

To whom or what have you given control of your happiness to? What steps can you take today to reclaim your happiness?

_____

_____

_____

_____

_____

_____

_____

_____

_____

_____

_____

_____

Day 225

You are a diamond! The source and essence of your being have existed for thousands of years, and no one can break you.

Note to myself   Date _____

What is your greatest strength? Have any of your recent actions demonstrated this strength?

_____

_____

_____

_____

_____

_____

_____

_____

_____

_____

_____

_____

_____

_____

Day 226

Resentment is often the result when you fail to set healthy boundaries.

Are you stubborn in your adherence to what you perceive as right or correct? Do you have to be right? Is your way better? Consider: How do you react when someone suggests they know a better way? Are you open to other's ideas, or do you stubbornly refuse to see their point of view? Allow yourself to be challenged every so often; it might just open new doors for you.

Note to myself   Date _____

How can you be more open to constructive feedback that could support you and your goals today?

_____

_____

_____

_____

_____

_____

_____

_____

_____

_____

Day 227

Taking responsibility for yourself and the choices that you've made is very empowering. The focus should never be on the mistakes you have made, rather knowing and understanding that you did your best at the time.

Now you have a new opportunity to make new and better choices. Sometimes it's just a matter of changing your method and allowing yourself to be flexible with new ideas.

Note to myself   Date _____

What steps can you take that will allow you to be more flexible in your life?

_____

_____

_____

_____

_____

_____

_____

_____

_____

_____

_____

_____

Day 228

It's time to let go of self-sabotage. "If I healed my old pain, what would change in my life as a result of this shift? What will change that I don't want to change?"

"Be empty of worrying. Think of who created thought! Why do you stay in prison, when the door is so wide open?" ~ *Rumi*

Note to myself   Date _____

Is the price you are paying for your pain worth it? What have you had enough of? What can you do today to bring positive changes in this area of your life?

_____

_____

_____

_____

_____

_____

_____

_____

_____

_____

_____

Day 229

Tension and energy in the body can move around.

It is often attracted to weak areas such as an injury. The body seems to have a way of distributing pain, mainly if the pain is not managed and dealt with immediately. When you suppress pain, whether it is emotional or physical, your body will let you know when it has reached its threshold. Physical pain does not just surface in the injured area; it can move into a different weaker area in the body. When you ignore the body's first initial message, it will create a new problem until you listen.

The cure for pain is in the pain." ~ Rumi

Note to myself   Date _____

Where in your life are you experiencing in the most emotional pain? What did you fail to do or say that could have solved this problem?

_____

_____

_____

_____

_____

_____

_____

_____

Day 230

One's identity can sometimes be tied-in so strongly with their trauma that the pain becomes a trophy—the story of their life.

Sometimes you need to be reminded how strong you are.

You have made it this far, and that speaks volumes about your inner strength and willpower!

I have spoken to many of my clients who said that if they don't have their trauma and pain to talk about, then they have nothing else to communicate.

You are not your pain; the pain was a passing experience. How you show up in life after the pain, that is what defines your identity. Sometimes you need to be reminded how strong you have been and still are!

Note to myself   Date _____

Success can be in your relationships, friendships, co-working relations, community or relationship with yourself. Where in your life have you failed to see the success that you have achieved?

_____

_____

_____

_____

_____

Day 231

When a person resolves secondary gains related to trauma, the body starts to remember how to complete trauma more easily, as no secondary gains are holding the trauma in place. It's called emotional freedom.

The wound is the place where the light enters you." ~ Rumi

Note to myself   Date _____

What's the wisest thing you have ever heard someone say? How can you apply that advice to your life today that would enable you to start your journey of emotional freedom?

_____

_____

_____

_____

_____

_____

_____

_____

_____

_____

_____

_____

_____

Day 232

Trust is not an action or a skill, but merely an intention where a person needs to feel safe enough to follow through on their intent to trust.

When you invest your time and energy in people, you are giving away precious moments of your life and time. Chose the people you spend time with wisely, leave no room for regrets.

Note to myself   Date _____

Truthfulness builds trust. How can you be more truthful with yourself today and why?

_____

_____

_____

_____

_____

_____

_____

_____

_____

_____

_____

_____

Day 233

This is what I call a beautiful domino effect! Everyone possesses the ability to heal. That ability can be reignited when key biological traumas are resolved.

Note to myself   Date _____

What is your biggest pain point in your life whether it's emotional or physical? Give the pain a voice, what would it say to you?

_____

_____

_____

_____

_____

_____

_____

_____

_____

_____

_____

_____

_____

_____

Day 234

You are a wealth of wisdom and your soul has the life span of the universe.

There is no positive benefit in undermining yourself.

Note to myself   Date _____

What makes a meaningful life? What can you start to do differently today that would bring forth these qualities in your life?

_____

_____

_____

_____

_____

_____

_____

_____

_____

_____

_____

_____

_____

_____

Day 235

Pretend that all of your abilities to be in control. Who are you now? What is your identity?

What is the worst thing that can happen if you let go of people and things in your life that does not require your energy and influence?

What are the fears that arise?

Are the fears real, or are they illusions? Focus on what matters in life and let the illusions drop away.

Break free from a prison that is not real.

"Let's ask God to help us to self-control for one who lacks it, lacks his grace." ~ Rumi

---

Note to myself   Date _____

I love this quote by Rumi, you are God and God is you. When you are truly coherent with your body and soul, then the journey of your life starts to flow like a river. There is no resistance, there is no need to control, it just flows as it is meant to. Being in control of your life is healthy, but when it robs you of your happiness and the ability to enjoy your life then there is an overcompensation that needs to be addressed.

_____

_____

_____

Day 236

If you don't know who you are, then how will others know?
Let your light shine and allow this to be what defines you and
contributes to who you transform into! You have more
potential than what you will ever come to realize!

"The world is a place where the light enters you." ~ Rumi

Note to myself   Date _____

Where in your life have you undermined your potential?

_____

_____

_____

_____

_____

_____

_____

_____

_____

_____

_____

_____

Day 237

When you allow your heart to open up to others, you allow true love and connections to form. Strong bonds are developed, and a deep understanding takes place that words cannot explain.

"Love is the bridge between you and everything." ~ Rumi

Note to myself   Date _____

In which area of your life are you blocking love from coming in and why?

What can you do differently today to allow love to knock on the door to your heart?

_____

_____

_____

_____

_____

_____

_____

_____

_____

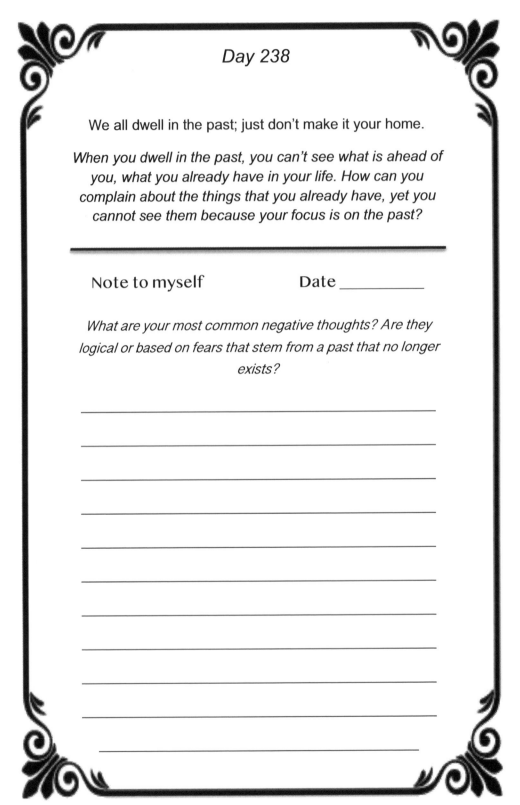

Day 238

We all dwell in the past; just don't make it your home.

When you dwell in the past, you can't see what is ahead of you, what you already have in your life. How can you complain about the things that you already have, yet you cannot see them because your focus is on the past?

Note to myself   Date _____

What are your most common negative thoughts? Are they logical or based on fears that stem from a past that no longer exists?

_____

_____

_____

_____

_____

_____

_____

_____

_____

_____

_____

Day 239

Life is not happening to you; you are having an experience.
If you don't like what you see, then you can change it.
Change doesn't always happen overnight, but the option to
make that change is still there. Are you ready to make that
change?

Note to myself   Date _____

*What in your life will change that you are not ready to change if
you did allow your self-limiting patterns to heal?*

_____

_____

_____

_____

_____

_____

_____

_____

_____

_____

_____

_____

Day 240

I am protected and empowered as I propel forward and towards my dreams!

Be kind to yourself, positively speak to yourself. Stop repeating negative words and judgments that were projected onto you by others who never even tried to get to know the real you! Keep moving forward.

Note to myself   Date _____

What do you need to believe in yourself in order to know that you can achieve your goals long-term and short-term goals?

_____

_____

_____

_____

_____

_____

_____

_____

_____

_____

_____

_____

_____

Day 241

Happiness is a decision!

Note to myself   Date _____

How can you simplify your life and focus on the most important things to you? It's time to declutter your life from habits, circumstances and relationships that continuously challenge your ability to create happiness in your life.

_____

_____

_____

_____

_____

_____

_____

_____

_____

_____

_____

_____

Day 242

You know that bucket list you have been dreaming about? It's time to start ticking the boxes. They are not going to tick themselves!

Note to myself   Date _____

What do you feel is preventing you from taking action? How can you act differently today that can kick start this process?

_____

_____

_____

_____

_____

_____

_____

_____

_____

_____

_____

_____

_____

Day 243

Those who don't believe in love will never find it.

Note to myself   Date _____

Write down 10 things that you love about yourself?

_____

_____

_____

_____

_____

_____

_____

_____

_____

_____

_____

_____

_____

_____

_____

_____

Day 244

A negative attitude will never give you a positive outcome!

Note to myself   Date _____

Write down your most dominant negative thoughts. Then write down the opposite positive thought of the negative thought. I invite you today to stay focused on the positive thoughts.

_____

_____

_____

_____

_____

_____

_____

_____

_____

_____

_____

_____

_____

_____

_____

Day 245

Stop looking for love if you still have the same patterns and baggage from your previous relationships. Find yourself, heal, and then let yourself shine. Let the next person see the best version of you.

Note to myself   Date _____

But first, how are you failing to see the best version of you?

_____

_____

_____

_____

_____

_____

_____

_____

_____

_____

_____

_____

_____

Day 246

A single word can open a heart. Be kind today; we are all fighting our own battles.

Note to myself   Date _____

How can you show kindness today?

How can you also show kindness to yourself?

_____

_____

_____

_____

_____

_____

_____

_____

_____

_____

_____

_____

Day 247

To the person who is reading this: Smile today, you are amazing as you are. There are people who love you. You don't always see it because your focus is elsewhere. Your efforts are valued.

Your purpose is important and has an impact and a ripple effect on another person's life. Without you, the world and someone else's world wouldn't be the same. You are important and good enough as you are.

Note to myself   Date _____

How have you failed recently to see your importance lately?

_____

_____

_____

_____

_____

_____

_____

_____

_____

_____

_____

Day 248

Holding on to pain is not one's purpose! It's a waste of precious time.

Note to myself   Date _____

How would your life be different if you let go of your painful past?

_____

_____

_____

_____

_____

_____

_____

_____

_____

_____

_____

_____

_____

Day 249

Sometimes death is not always the most significant loss. It could also be when that something special inside of you dies when you still had time to fix it but never did. Never leave room for regret in your life!

Note to myself   Date _____

What do you regret in your life? What can you do differently today to avoid more regretful moments?

_____

_____

_____

_____

_____

_____

_____

_____

_____

_____

_____

_____

Day 250

While a person may be unable to access positive emotions due to stress, they still can feel these emotions. It's called inner resources. Are you ready to awaken yours?

Your mind is powerful. When you invest your time and energy in positive thoughts, then they are the seeds that will start to grow.

Note to myself   Date _____

Write down 10 positive emotions and thoughts that you want to feel and access again. I invite you start by holding these positive states of mind. Go into the day as if though you already fully possess these positive resources.

_____

_____

_____

_____

_____

_____

_____

_____

_____

_____

_____

Day 251

We sometimes learn to feel comfortable feeling uncomfortable. Where in your life have you fallen into that trap? When you realize that you have perhaps fallen into this pattern, find creative ways to set yourself free.

You are not meant to be in one place; you are meant to play in life. Live big, love in big and deep ways and leave a legacy behind that will last an eternity.

"Freedom is what the heart wants, regardless of the opinions of others." ~ Paulo Coelho

Note to myself   Date _____

What can you do differently today that will allow you to feel emotionally free in your life?

_____

_____

_____

_____

_____

_____

_____

_____

_____

Day 252

I am connected and coherent with the energetic force that created me.

Just because things don't always work out the way you envisioned, doesn't mean that you are not on the right path.

"Straight roads do not make skillful drivers." ~ Paulo Coelho

Note to myself   Date _____

What do you feel most disconnected from in your life right now? What can you do differently today that will allow you to reconnect back to this missing link?

_____

_____

_____

_____

_____

_____

_____

_____

_____

_____

_____

Day 253

As a friend, lover, colleague, or facilitator, never become too attached to the outcome of the support you provide to someone. Know that what you have done was good enough.

You are a beacon of light, just as you are. Know that you are good enough and that your efforts to help and support another is good enough. Sometimes we are given just enough resources to help another. You don't want to disempower them; you want to remind them how strong they are and what they are capable of.

Note to myself   Date _____

Who in your life needs your support right now? How can you support them without sacrificing your own limits?

_____

_____

_____

_____

_____

_____

_____

_____

_____

Day 254

I have had enough of "circumstances," from now on, I only create opportunities that will set me free!

You are not a prisoner in your life. Your life is not a misery. You are not lost. Your path forward is not unbeknown to you. What you seemed to have forgotten was how to be creative with your goals and strategies.

Note to myself   Date _____

When do you feel most creative? Do more of that and when you are in that creative state, brain storm new strategies and solutions to challenging problems in your life. If there is a will there is a way.

_____

_____

_____

_____

_____

_____

_____

_____

_____

_____

Day 255

Never assume that you think you know how someone else feels. What is upsetting for them might be a completely different experience for you. Today is judgment-free day.

Have patience and compassion today to try and understand why someone is perhaps acting out of character. Why they are upset because of something that happened that probably would have been nothing to you. Sometimes just a little bit of understanding and compassion can heal a broken heart.

Note to myself   Date _____

In which aspect of your life do you need to show more kindness and compassion towards yourself?

_____

_____

_____

_____

_____

_____

_____

_____

_____

_____

_____

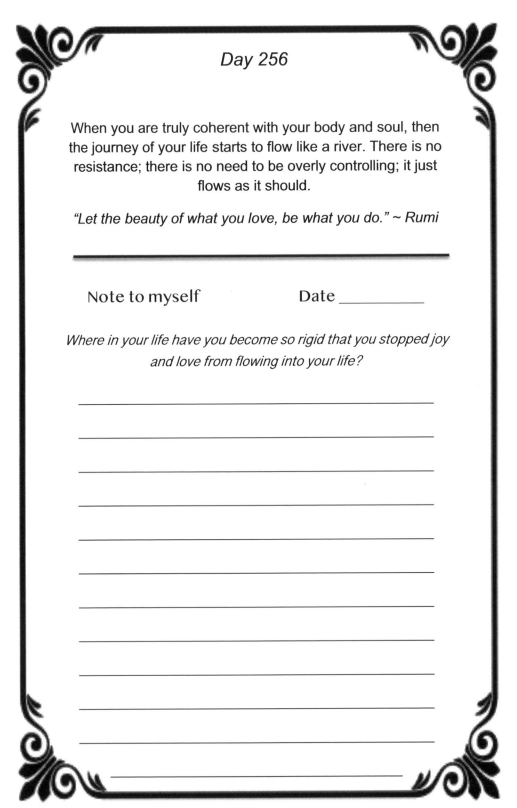

Day 256

When you are truly coherent with your body and soul, then the journey of your life starts to flow like a river. There is no resistance; there is no need to be overly controlling; it just flows as it should.

"Let the beauty of what you love, be what you do." ~ Rumi

Note to myself   Date _____

Where in your life have you become so rigid that you stopped joy and love from flowing into your life?

_____

_____

_____

_____

_____

_____

_____

_____

_____

_____

_____

Day 257

You were meant to be free.

Your destiny belongs to you. Your goals belong to you. You can share them with others, however, the only person that will set the wheel in motion is you.

You are the driver and the one that can make anything happen if you stay focused and within a place of clarity. Never make a decision when in doubt. Never answer when you are not sure. Never make a promise you can't keep. By being loyal to yourself, you become loyal to your future and others. It sets you free from unnecessary obligations. Remember, you were meant to be free!

Note to myself   Date _____

In which aspect of your life do you need to give yourself more freedom? What steps can you take today to bring you closer to that sense of freedom?

_____

_____

_____

_____

_____

_____

_____

Day 258

Soul searching is not meant to be painful, it's; supposed to be a journey where you allow yourself to move into a a place where you can hear your inner voice and the song that sings you home.

A healing journey is not meant to be painful. It's not meant to rob you of your quality of life.

It's not meant to cause you to lose sight of what used to make you happy. Your healing journey is intended to take you back to your true authentic self.

Note to myself   Date _____

Where in your life are you pushing yourself too hard? How can you be kinder and gentler on yourself today?

_____

_____

_____

_____

_____

_____

_____

_____

_____

_____

Day 259

Have the patience and compassion today to try and understand why someone is perhaps acting out of character. Sometimes just a little bit of understanding and compassion can heal a broken heart.

"Listen with ears of tolerance. See through eyes of compassion. Speak with the language of love." ~ Rumi

---

Note to myself   Date _____

In which aspect of your life can you be more patient with yourself?

_____

_____

_____

_____

_____

_____

_____

_____

_____

_____

_____

_____

Day 260

Ever thought about how you can help change the world? Why not love yourself so much that you become a source of inspiration to people?

Let your words and actions of love and kindness have such a strong ripple effect into someone else's broken heart.

Your mission today, if you choose to accept it, is to show kindness, patience, and love. You don't always know what is going on in someone else's life. Someone else's pain is often unbeknown to us. Your actions and words might be the soothing comfort that another might need today.

Note to myself   Date _____

Kind of encouragement did you need during your challenging times? How can you give that to yourself today?

_____

_____

_____

_____

_____

_____

_____

_____

_____

Day 261

An open heart knows the language of love and innocence.

"Love, the supreme musician, is always playing in our souls."
~ Rumi

Note to myself   Date _____

We can't always be great at everything, but we can be great at love. First, you have to love yourself. What can you do differently today to improve your relationship with yourself?

_____

_____

_____

_____

_____

_____

_____

_____

_____

_____

_____

_____

Day 262

Stop playing it small; your actions are part of a collective movement that keeps the universe alive and flowing.

Enough said! Keep moving forward, your soul and the universe has got your back.

Note to myself   Date _____

How can you allow more support to come into your life today?

_____

_____

_____

_____

_____

_____

_____

_____

_____

_____

_____

_____

_____

Day 263

Secondary gains are unconscious motivators that reward people in one way or another for holding on to their problems. When a bad habit serves a person, there is an unconscious benefit that starts to form.

These hidden benefits can become debilitating, but only if you give your power away to it. You choose where your energy flows. Are you ready to take it back?

Note to myself   Date _____

In which area of your life do you need to take your power back?
In which area of your life do you need to implement it more?

_____

_____

_____

_____

_____

_____

_____

_____

_____

_____

_____

Day 264

Did you know that womb stress takes place when the mother of the baby experiences a great deal of stress or shock or experiences repetitive negative emotions such as anger or feeling abused? This is where an identity overlap between mother and child starts.

Affirmation today: "I am free to change how I respond to the world."

Note to myself   Date _____

Which characteristics to you share with your mother? Are they empowering you or sabotaging you? What is the hidden benefit of holding onto the sabotaging aspects? Meaning, what in your life will change that you are not ready to change if you did heal the sabotaging patterns that do not belong to you?

_____

_____

_____

_____

_____

_____

_____

_____

_____

Day 265

Your destiny has more than one option, be creative with it!

"Live life as though everything is rigged in your favor!" ~ Rumi

Note to myself   Date _____

What kind of mindset do you need to have today in order to feel successful and accomplished in your life?

_____

_____

_____

_____

_____

_____

_____

_____

_____

_____

_____

_____

_____

Day 266

Shame is just an emotion. You are not the origin of shame.

Shame is the result of how a situation made you feel; every emotion and belief that follows are part of a ripple effect.

Note to myself   Date _____

Shame is not your identity. What do you need to believe in yourself in order to know that you are worthy and good enough?

_____

_____

_____

_____

_____

_____

_____

_____

_____

_____

_____

_____

_____

Day 267

Love and acceptance should not be tied to doing chores,
sacrificing your values and self-respect.

"The only lasting beauty is the beauty of the heart." ~ Rumi

Note to myself   Date _____

*Are you doing too much for loved ones? What can you do for
yourself today to emotionally and spiritually invest more in
yourself?*

_____

_____

_____

_____

_____

_____

_____

_____

_____

_____

_____

_____

_____

Day 268

You are a diamond. You are already valuable, brilliant and, unique in your own right. Sometimes you need a buff and polish to bring out that natural brilliance and clarity within yourself.

The best part is when you start to see that beautiful side within yourself.

Note to myself   Date _____

_____

_____

_____

_____

_____

_____

_____

_____

_____

_____

_____

_____

_____

Day 269

When you start to process your past and move forward with your life, it is important that it is a conscious decision you've made. This decision should never be made on your behalf.

Your whole heart and soul should be in it. You should want the change. No one can push you into a direction that is not coherent with your soul's path. Learn to listen, you will know where it is that you need to be, right here, right now.

Note to myself   Date _____

How did you fail to listen to yourself recently? What steps can you take next time to avoid this?

_____

_____

_____

_____

_____

_____

_____

_____

_____

_____

_____

Day 270

The essence of who you are is permanent. The worst thing that can happen to your essence is that it becomes suppressed.

You are invalidating your power by thinking that it has been taken away from you.

"What you seek, is seeking you." ~ Rumi

Note to myself   Date _____

What do you need to believe in yourself in order to know that all the answers are already within you?

_____

_____

_____

_____

_____

_____

_____

_____

_____

_____

_____

Day 271

The more your true authentic-self shines, the more people in your circle start to move and change in positive ways.

"When you let go of who you are, you become who you might be." ~ Rumi

Note to myself   Date _____

Who in your life is your role model? What inspires you about them? What does this person believe about themselves that allow them to be the person that they are? How can you incorporate that believe system in your life in a way that is compatible with you?

_____

_____

_____

_____

_____

_____

_____

_____

_____

_____

_____

Day 272

I will have all that my heart desires.

The only way that you will never attract what you want is when you stop believing.

Note to myself   Date _____

Write down your greatest desire. What steps can you take today to feel the feeling of your wish fulfilled?

_____

_____

_____

_____

_____

_____

_____

_____

_____

_____

_____

_____

_____

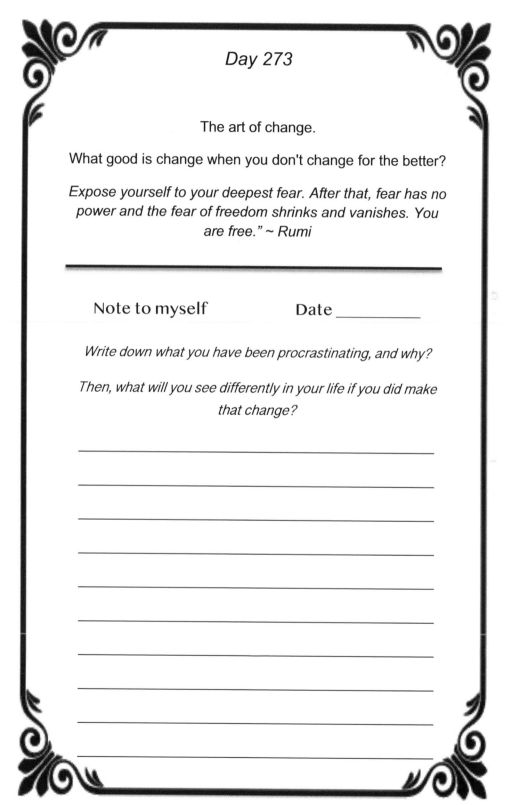

Day 273

The art of change.

What good is change when you don't change for the better?

Expose yourself to your deepest fear. After that, fear has no power and the fear of freedom shrinks and vanishes. You are free." ~ Rumi

Note to myself   Date _____

Write down what you have been procrastinating, and why?

Then, what will you see differently in your life if you did make that change?

_____

_____

_____

_____

_____

_____

_____

_____

_____

_____

Day 274

You have been running away for too long. It's time to find rest and peace. It's time to enjoy your efforts, no matter how big or small they may seem. Success is in the eye of the beholder.

Note to myself   Date _____

Write down what you are most proud of in your life today?

_____

_____

_____

_____

_____

_____

_____

_____

_____

_____

_____

_____

_____

Day 275

Pursuing a goal or person that is not meant for your path will only disappoint your expectations.

Learn to recognize what is right for you, who and what will help your soul grow. Who and what will enrich your path and dreams? Awareness of yourself and your boundaries will shed light on the way forward.

Note to myself   Date _____

Where in your life have you abandoned your goals and why?

What small steps can you take today restart this process?

_____

_____

_____

_____

_____

_____

_____

_____

_____

_____

_____

Day 276

Let go of what no longer serves you and do what brings you peace.

You always have a choice.

Note to myself   Date _____

Write down 5 things that bring you peace in your life.

_____

_____

_____

_____

_____

_____

_____

_____

_____

_____

_____

_____

_____

_____

Day 277

I'm telling my story in its entirety to show you that you can heal, even when negative patterns have been set over years and lifetimes.

Your past can control who you are until you find your voice.

"You are not a drop in the ocean, you are the entire ocean in a drop." ~ Rumi

Note to myself   Date _____

Write down five strengths that you have.

_____

_____

_____

_____

_____

_____

_____

_____

_____

_____

_____

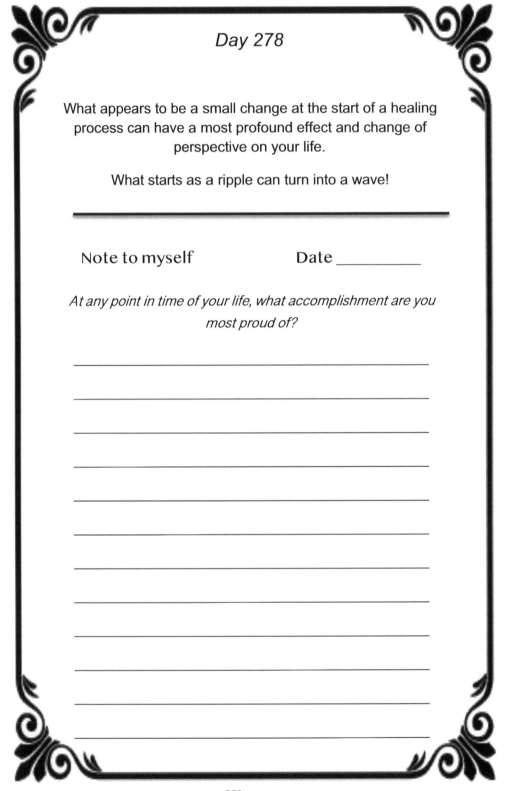

Day 278

What appears to be a small change at the start of a healing process can have a most profound effect and change of perspective on your life.

What starts as a ripple can turn into a wave!

Note to myself   Date _____

At any point in time of your life, what accomplishment are you most proud of?

_____

_____

_____

_____

_____

_____

_____

_____

_____

_____

_____

_____

Day 279

Any change in the right direction is a positive step forward, no matter how big or small the adjustment.

It is essential to learn how to readjust your energy levels and how much you are going to emotionally and energetically invest in people and projects. Love yourself enough to know where your limits and are. Keep the balance.

Note to myself   Date _____

Where in your life do you feel out of balance? What smalls steps can you take today to bring more balance?

_____

_____

_____

_____

_____

_____

_____

_____

_____

_____

Day 280

You can never change people. You can only change yourself with the intention that it will revolutionize your relationships with others and how you respond to the impact of these relationships.

"Set your life on fire. Seek those who fan your flames."
~ Rumi

Note to myself   Date _____

Who in your life have you been trying to change? What can you change in within yourself that would allow you to let go of needing to change someone else?

_____

_____

_____

_____

_____

_____

_____

_____

_____

_____

_____

_____

_____

Day 281

Love is unconditional; love is respect, it's compassion and understanding. It's when you can love someone while they make mistakes. It's when you can see the truth behind someone's pain and anger. Love is what lasts even when circumstances and people have left your life.

Love is like energy, energy doesn't have a beginning, and it doesn't have an end. It's always alive.

Note to myself   Date _____

What steps can you take today to reignite love for yourself?
What action towards yourself will allow you to feel loved?

_____

_____

_____

_____

_____

_____

_____

_____

_____

_____

_____

Day 282

Allow others to see your true authentic self. There is no higher vibration and level of honesty.

Are you ready to be you?

Note to myself   Date _____

How do you think others see you?

What do you need to believe in yourself in order to feel confident and strong within yourself regardless of another's opinion of you?

Day 283

Without healthy boundaries, you lack a strong foundation within yourself, your life, your environment, and your relationships. Know where your limits are.

"While the mind sees only boundaries, love knows the secret way there." ~ Rumi

Note to myself   Date _____

Write down at least five boundary values that are important to you. For example, you know you're your boundaries are being overstepped when you experience the below 5 reactions:

_____

_____

_____

_____

_____

_____

_____

_____

_____

_____

_____

_____

Day 284

We all have been in pain. Some of us have experienced it to its fullest extent. It either broke you or caused you to make decisions in your life that didn't serve your journey. But it doesn't mean that it has to control your future and who you want to become.

The result of a great of stress is often confusion, lack of trust, and resentment towards people who were meant to look out for you. Feeling unstable and lacking a proper foundation on which to build your future. Suppression and anger become your power tools to survive and inevitably, your passion, joy, freedom, love, and personality slowly become suppressed.

Note to myself   Date _____

You are powerful and strong enough to heal this, you have come this far already. You might as well go all the way. What do you need to believe in yourself in order to know that you can set yourself free from pain and stress in your life?

_____

_____

_____

_____

_____

_____

_____

_____

Day 285

When you blame your past for how you feel, then you keep reinforcing the fact that your past circumstances have the upper hand. It also means that your history has complete control over your emotions, how you express yourself, and how you live your life.

When you take responsibility for yourself, you take your negative circumstances and an abuser's power away. You immediately stop being a victim of circumstance. You step into your power, regain your sense of self, and ultimately become the driving force behind your happiness and success.

Note to myself   Date _____

Taking responsibility means taking control of your future. Where in your life do you feel you have lost control? What steps can you take today to take your power back?

_____

_____

_____

_____

_____

_____

_____

_____

Day 286

I decided to change, I decided to take my power back, and I decided to be free and innocent again!

You are the creator of your movie, you are the driver of your vehicle, and you are the dictator of your show.

Note to myself   Date _____

Have you stopped being playful in your life? In which aspect of your life do you need to be more playful and why?

_____

_____

_____

_____

_____

_____

_____

_____

_____

_____

_____

_____

Day 287

It is essential to understand that your freedom and innocence are not taken away from you. It can never be taken away by anyone. You have allowed that part of you to be suppressed, a part of you that is perfect and divine. It is meant to shine!

Often your freedom and innocence can become suppressed as circumstances in your life had changed. You had to adapt to an environment in which there was no place for the expression of freedom and innocence. I Invite you to realize now, that those circumstances no longer exist. You have the power to change it 360 degrees around! Are you ready?

Note to myself   Date _____

I invite you today to embody and hold the mindset of being and feeling free in your life. It is after all your birthright.

_____

_____

_____

_____

_____

_____

_____

_____

Day 288

If you couldn't exercise your boundaries as a child, then how are you supposed to exercise your boundaries as an adult? Do you overcompensate or are you the peacekeeper?

Balance is key! The better you get to know yourself, the healthier your actions and reactions will become.

Note to myself   Date _____

How well do express your boundaries? What steps can you take today that would allow you to reclaim your boundaries without having to fight for it?

_____

_____

_____

_____

_____

_____

_____

_____

_____

_____

_____

Day 289

Remember, you experience stress on a biological level, not on a spiritual level. Do not let your circumstances define who you are and who you become.

You are a perfect being, but sometimes you are slowed down by past challenging experiences. The question is, do these past experiences still affect you? Let them go and once you have done that, keep doing it

Note to myself   Date _____

What would your future look like if your past no longer held you back?

_____

_____

_____

_____

_____

_____

_____

_____

_____

_____

_____

_____

Day 290

Shame is just an emotion. You are not the origin of shame. Shame is the result of how a situation made you feel.

We feel shame when we are made to think that we failed to meet someone's expectations. Often those expectations were projected because the projector couldn't meet the standards they were setting for themselves. People usually try to live and complete their dreams through others, and failure for them was not an option. Make sure that your actions are driven by your desires and personal goals and not someone else's.

Note to myself   Date _____

Have you abandoned your goals for the sake of helping someone else achieve theirs? What steps can you take today to bring balance back into your life?

_____

_____

_____

_____

_____

_____

_____

_____

Day 291

Do you remember the challenging times when you wished and prayed for the things that you have now?

Note to myself   Date _____

Write down 5 things that you are most grateful for today?

_____

_____

_____

_____

_____

_____

_____

_____

_____

_____

_____

_____

_____

_____

_____

_____

Day 292

When you start to heal from your past, it is essential that it is a conscious decision you've made. This decision should never be made on your behalf.

Your whole heart and soul should be in it. Your commitment to change is what will lead you on a journey of transformation.

"Let yourself be silently drawn by the strange pull of what you really love. It will not lead you astray." ~ Rumi

Note to myself   Date _____

What negative belief, pattern, habit or person do you consciously choose to let go of today?

_____

_____

_____

_____

_____

_____

_____

_____

_____

_____

Day 293

The essence of who you are is permanent. The worst thing that can happen to your essence is that it becomes suppressed. It lies dormant, waiting to be rediscovered.

You are invalidating your power by thinking that it has been taken away from you. I invite you today to become aware of the part of you that is divinely perfect.

Note to myself   Date _____

Complete this sentence: I am perfect just as I am and...

_____

_____

_____

_____

_____

_____

_____

_____

_____

_____

_____

Day 294

Your destiny is to meet your true authentic self. It is to express love and kindness and to be a beacon of light to those who are in need of love and support.

Being in pain is not your life purpose or destiny. You are meant to be free.

Note to myself   Date _____

What steps can you take to show kindness to yourself today?

_____

_____

_____

_____

_____

_____

_____

_____

_____

_____

_____

_____

_____

Day 295

Seeking revenge only serves to hurt you even more. Seeking revenge takes you away from your path, which has so much more meaning and potential.

A destiny that has no bounds is waiting for you. Choose how you spend your time and energy wisely. Needing to seek revenge means that you have lost faith and trust in the cycle of life and karma.

Note to myself   Date _____

In which aspect of your life has resentment taken over? What steps can you take today that will allow you to set yourself free from this cycle?

_____

_____

_____

_____

_____

_____

_____

_____

_____

_____

_____

Day 296

When you find your inner peace, the chaos and violence of the world will no longer sway you from your destiny.

We were not designed to be violent or harvest hatred and resentment towards one another. If we were created to hold onto these negative emotions, then why are so many people suffering from ailments? It only chips away at a once peaceful world and state of mind.

Note to myself   Date _____

What steps can you take today to restore your inner peace?

_____

_____

_____

_____

_____

_____

_____

_____

_____

_____

_____

Day 297

People only respect you as much as you respect yourself—it always starts within.

"There is no respect for others without humility in one's self."
~ Henri Frederic Amiel

How people treat you is often a reflection of how you treat yourself. You are disrespecting yourself by being in a relationship where you feel disrespected. You are disrespecting yourself by not saying no when you know you should have. You are disrespecting yourself by not expressing your self-worth. You might find yourself in stressful circumstances or where you feel disrespected.

Note to myself   Date _____

If you can relate to this then I have to ask you this question, "Why are you abusing yourself by allowing this?"

_____

_____

_____

_____

_____

_____

_____

_____

Day 298

Freedom and innocence is only a decision away. No one can rob you of a state of mind that you always had access to. It's only a matter of remembering how to access it again.

"I have decided to stick with love. Hate is too great a burden to bear." Martin Luther King, Jr.

Note to myself   Date _____

What is burdening you today? What steps can you take today to lessen the impact of this burden?

_____

_____

_____

_____

_____

_____

_____

_____

_____

_____

_____

_____

Day 299

Help someone because you want to and not because you expect something in return. An act of kindness can take 2 minutes out of your day and change the world for someone else.

Note to myself   Date _____

In which area of your life can you show more kindness today?

_____

_____

_____

_____

_____

_____

_____

_____

_____

_____

_____

_____

_____

Day 300

Taking personal responsibility does not mean that someone who caused you harm will get away with their actions. It doesn't mean that the past will be forgotten.

It only means that you are consciously taking your power back, standing strong again, and empowered throughout your journey. When taking personal responsibility, you are ultimately taking charge of your future and emotional state. Taking personal responsibility = taking control of a situation that was once out of control. It's an incredibly powerful move to make, are you ready?

Note to myself   Date _____

How can you implement this concept and suggestion in your life today?

_____

_____

_____

_____

_____

_____

_____

_____

_____

Day 301

Your only limit is what you think you are capable of.

Note to myself   Date _____

Write down 5 limitations that you feel you have. Then, write down what you need to believe in yourself in order to know that you can overcome these perceived limitations?

_____

_____

_____

_____

_____

_____

_____

_____

_____

_____

_____

_____

_____

_____

Day 302

Your past is merely a story now. It is not real anymore. You are keeping it alive by holding on to pain. Injustice has transformed into anger.

Has the anger now become your driving force to fight through life and circumstances? You cannot find peace when anger is your motivator. You cannot be happy when anger has taken its place.

Peace cannot be achieved when anger is the driver. Anger attracts anger.

What do you want to pursue today? What do you choose to pursue in the long term?

Be mindful where you invest your energy.

It could be the answer as to why you are faced with challenges.

Anger is the end result of feeling out of control and feeling as if though you have lost power in a situation or even in your life.

Note to myself   Date _____

The question is why do you feel this way? What can you do to change this? There is an abundance of answers, the filters through which we see the world is what often sabotages us from seeing the answers that are right in front of us.

_____

_____

Day 303

You are a human being and a sacred soul who is meant to be in harmony with yourself, your environment and with all that is.

In today's society, that state of mind can be challenging to achieve due to the stress and conflict that you are facing. When pain is inflicted it's often hard not to have the desire to cause that same amount of pain onto another. You might often feel it's your duty to teach them a lesson, and yes, there are cases where steps need to be taken to bring justice where it's needed.

Note to myself   Date _____

Today I invite you to explore and clearly discern when to take a step back and when to act. Allow this to become part of your practice today. Let go of anger, anger and hatred has never brought peace. Anger has never been the beginning of a peaceful solution.

_____

_____

_____

_____

_____

_____

_____

Day 304

Always make a decision that your future self will be grateful for.

Note to myself   Date _____

What positive action can you take today that your future self will be grateful for?

_____

_____

_____

_____

_____

_____

_____

_____

_____

_____

_____

_____

_____

_____

_____

Day 305

Your willingness to change your life and to move away from your past should be so fearless that you show those who lost their way how it's done.

When you decide to change and heal, you will be amazed at the support that will manifest on your path.

Opportunities and circumstances will come forward that will support and reward your decision to heal.

You might lose a couple of friends and alliances along the way.

Be okay with that; it's not that you have outgrown them, you have not become better than them, the direction of your path has changed to a different route.

Note to myself   Date _____

Be confident and feel strong within yourself, it's motivating and admirable for people to see how much you can change. It just might re-ignite their fearlessness to move forward in life and to break free from self-sabotaging patterns.

_____

_____

_____

_____

_____

_____

Day 306

You can't beat someone who never gives up.

Which side of the line are you on?

Note to myself   Date _____

Do you feel defeated today? What steps can you take today to take your power back from a perceived failure?

_____
_____
_____
_____
_____
_____
_____
_____
_____
_____
_____
_____
_____
_____
_____

Day 307

Who have you become? Painful events are only something that happened to you. It is not part of your identity.

Who you are at a core level of existence is perfect, innocent, beautiful, and stronger than what you can ever imagine!

Note to myself   Date _____

Write down one aspect of yourself that you feel has been changed and shaped by physical or emotional pain. What do you need to believe in yourself in order to know that this block that you feel is not part of your true authentic self?

_____

_____

_____

_____

_____

_____

_____

_____

_____

_____

_____

Day 308

Be and feel inspired today. You are in control of how you feel, reclaim your power, and choose to have a great day today.

I invite you today to stop giving your power away and your ability to experience and feel joy and freedom.

No one should ever have that level of control over your emotional state and happiness. You can, and should, be the driver of this aspect of your life, amongst many.

It doesn't matter whether you are at work, home, or in the middle of a storm. You are stronger than you realize. Look back on your life with victory; you have made it so far. You are a better and stronger person today.

No one can take away the emotional strength that you have gained and the teachings that you have had.

Note to myself   Date _____

Write down five or more of your greatest strengths.

_____

_____

_____

_____

_____

_____

Day 309

React to every vibe and tribe that excites your soul; this is how you find your passion and the road that will lead you to happiness.

_____

Note to myself   Date _____

Write down five things that make you happy. What steps can you take today to create more of these happy moments in your life?

_____

_____

_____

_____

_____

_____

_____

_____

_____

_____

_____

_____

_____

_____

Day 310

People often become so competitive that it robs them of their humanity, and that is a lonely place to be.

Become aware today where your focus is. Is it on your success? Is it to get that big promotion? Is it to become better than your competitor? Take a few minutes today to remind yourself why you started your goals in the first place. Remember to be kind along your path of success.

Note to myself   Date _____

Take yourself back to the time when you were enthusiastic about your goals and shared your excitement about it with those around you. What did it look and feel like?

_____

_____

_____

_____

_____

_____

_____

_____

_____

Day 311

Out with the old and in with the new! What new changes are you going to make in your life today that can instantly improve your quality of life?

Be creative, be a problem solver. Most importantly of all, be your OWN problem solver.

Do you always wait for someone to give you the answer?

Do you always wait for someone to intervene and save the day?

Be your savior, be your problem solver.

Brainstorm methods, be in control of the technique and make sure that the next step will be complimentary to your path.

Never place the path and way forward of your destiny in someone else's hands.

Note to myself   Date _____

Write down a note to your future self. What should your future self be more aware of? How can you incorporate the answer that you wrote down in your life right now?

_____

_____

_____

_____

Day 312

I love who I am and have become, nothing that anyone can say or do will sway me from my path.

Love yourself and respect your needs and values. Just because others don't understand your path or your intentions doesn't mean that you should give up.

It only means that the company you entertain has not taken the time to try to understand. Be okay with that. Move forward, fearlessly.

The right people who will support your cause will show up at the right time.

Just because you feel you need people who you can relate to your path means that you are undermining your ability to achieve these goals on your own.

Note to myself   Date _____

How can you be more supportive toward yourself while are you are achieving your goals today?

_____

_____

_____

_____

_____

_____

Day 313

I release myself from being a victim of people's anger and harsh words.

Have you ever entertained the thought and realization that you do not have to carry the pain of another's anger and harsh words that were projected onto you?

Have you ever thought that, in most cases, it's just merely their way of crying out for help?

Has that anger become their best defense?

It's their default. When this person feel they are losing control of a situation or feel unheard, they revert to a type of behavior that allows them to be heard, listened to and respected.

Although they demand respect, they haven't earned it. They fight for it. They induce fear in people to establish their presence and authority.

Note to myself   Date _____

You can't build lasting friendships and relations with colleagues in this way. Today, if someone projects anger towards you, I invite you to see beyond the anger and the words that are being expressed. What is being said is often completely unrelated to what is being experienced within them. Write down what you truly felt the last time when you were angry. What did you feel before you felt angry?

Day 314

Taking responsibility means that you take your power back and take charge of your future.

Your future and success are not in the hands of others anymore! The ball is now in your court.

Note to myself   Date _____

Does your life feel chaotic lately? Where do you need to bring your focus back to? What distracted you from your focus in the first place?

_____

_____

_____

_____

_____

_____

_____

_____

_____

_____

_____

_____

Day 315

Do you feel overburdened by responsibilities today? Whose responsibility are you taking responsibility for? Let go of responsibilities that do not belong to you.

Why do you feel responsible for responsibilities that do not belong to you or concern you?

Often we try to determine our self-worth by how much we can do for others.

Do you feel valued and important when you are needed and as a result give too much because you don't value your time and energy?

Have discernment about what is and what is not your problem and responsibilities today.

Where are you overextending yourself, and how can you correct it by finding balance again?

Love yourself enough to have healthy boundaries and love yourself enough to express them with kindness.

Note to myself   Date _____

I ask you again, "What is the benefit of being responsible for other peoples' problems?" No benefit? Then what steps can you take today to lessen this burden? If there are benefits, what are they and are they worth it?

_____

_____

Day 316

Let every day be a new day. Make new decisions, make adjustments, and make changes. It doesn't matter how big or small the decision or change is, what does matter is that you never give up.

When we become rigid and stagnant, we become stuck. We lose our passion; we stop nurturing the things in life that once brought us joy and happiness. It is so important to keep being creative when you run into a problem.

A problem only signals to you that a different method to what you are doing is needed.

Be flexible, just because a temporary change in direction is not what you wanted, doesn't mean that it's not going to get you to where you want to be.

Keep making healthy changes and adjustments to your life.

Keep moving forward and keep the pace and momentum you achieved alive by reminding yourself why you started this journey in the first place.

Note to myself   Date _____

Why did you start your biggest goal?

_____

_____

_____

_____

Day 317

When you feel angry today, become aware of how you truly feel. Anger is a symptom of a much deeper emotional battle from the past that may not be resolved.

Today, focus on how you feel instead of focusing on the symptoms of your emotions. What is underneath the anger? That is the emotion that should be expressed, express how you truly feel so that people can understand your needs better, and work towards a resolution and not conflict.

Note to myself   Date _____

What is frustrating you today? What do you need to communicate to either yourself or another in order to bring balance back into your life?

_____

_____

_____

_____

_____

_____

_____

_____

Day 318

Who you are and what you do is good enough. There are always people who appreciate what you do.

The only obstacle is that you don't always get to see how much these people value you!

The message for today is to start valuing yourself so that you don't have that deeply hidden need to seek validation from anyone in any way.

I invite you today to become aware of all the good things you have done for others and yourself.

Know that what you have done has incredible value in it. You took action because there was a need and you fulfilled that need, whether it was for yourself or someone else.

Become aware that sometimes we focus more on serving others, instead of finding a balance between our needs and the needs of others.

Note to myself   Date _____

Write down 10 things that you have done for someone else that you feel satisfied with.

_____

_____

_____

_____

Day 319

You can only be a victim by choice. Who do you choose to be today?

You were born free. It's your birthright to be free.

Note to myself   Date _____

Freedom is being you without anyone's permission. Whose permission do you need to be and feel free and why?

_____

_____

_____

_____

_____

_____

_____

_____

_____

_____

_____

_____

_____

_____

Day 320

You are surrounded by everything that you were and have become.

If you energize negativity, then it will show up in your life.

If you energize positivity, then it will show up in your life.

If you energize love, then that will show up too….. I know … you might be saying that you have been doing this, but nothing happens.

Have you ever thought that if you have a negative association with, let's say, love?

You try to energize and focus on love in your life then you might still end up attracting unhealthy love?

Become aware of where thoughts originate from and how much you energize them.

Note to myself   Date _____

Write down your definition of love

_____

_____

_____

_____

_____

_____

Day 321

Reclaim your inner child, reclaim your innocence, you grow old before your time when you fail to delve deep and rediscover that part of you that wants to play and be creative.

When was the last time you had fun? I mean genuinely had fun, the kind of joy when you forgot who was watching?

That you are oblivious to people's judgment? Think back to a time when you experienced this.

We all have had a moment like this, even if it was just for a few seconds. I invite you today to find that time and recreate those fun moments.

Even if you sit in silence and meditate for a few minutes and find that moment, that moment of joy, fun, and freedom.

Note to myself   Date _____

Write down your fondest memory when you felt carefree and playful?

_____

_____

_____

_____

_____

Day 322

Equality is an experience that is right there in front of you. Equality can become a state of mind and have a positive ripple effect on your self-esteem.

How you show up in your life is what defines the rest.

We all have equal rights, yet we undermine our self-worth and often end up pulling the short end of the rope.

Some religions and cultures rob people from this god-given right.

Some of us might find ourselves in situations where we don't have an option other than playing small.

However, the power behind this message is that equality can become a state of mind and have a positive ripple effect on your self-esteem.

Note to myself   Date _____

It can change how you feel about yourself. Don't let your circumstances control and rob you of something that you can control. No one can take away your power to control how you feel. Is this true for you today? If not, why?

_____

_____

_____

_____

Day 323

When the day comes that you learn to love fearlessly and deeply, that is the day when hate becomes just a word.

No one is perfect, we all have our good days and bad days. We have moments of patience and moments of impatience.

We have a fear of love and then we have a moment when we love so deeply that we become scared.

Hatred and resentment have become an unconscious boundary for so many of us, to protect ourselves.

No one likes feeling vulnerable.

What happened to you when you opened up for the first time to love?

Perhaps your heart was broken.

The secret is that holding onto hatred and anger will not help you to attract love again.

Hatred attracts hatred, people, and circumstances that create situations that cause you to feel hate.

Note to myself   Date _____

Let go of old challenges and pain from the past. This is what is stopping you from loving deeply. It stops you from inviting healthy love into your life. Are you ready to take the leap? What do you need to let go of in order to love again?

_____

_____

_____

Day 324

Even when you are battling in the middle of a storm, you can go within and find the peace that you need.

Take a break, take a breath, be still, and even stop if you need to. Regroup emotionally, spiritually, and mentally.

Set clear intentions every day and have a clear structure set out for your day.

When you have a clear intention and structure, then no amount of chaos can sway you from achieving your goals.

If you feel you have moved away from your path, then find that clear intention you originally had, find structure again.

Note to myself   Date _____

Rediscover the state of mind that you had when you started out, before the challenges started. Stay focused and connected to that. So there are three steps: clear intention, structure and stay focused.

_____

_____

_____

_____

_____

_____

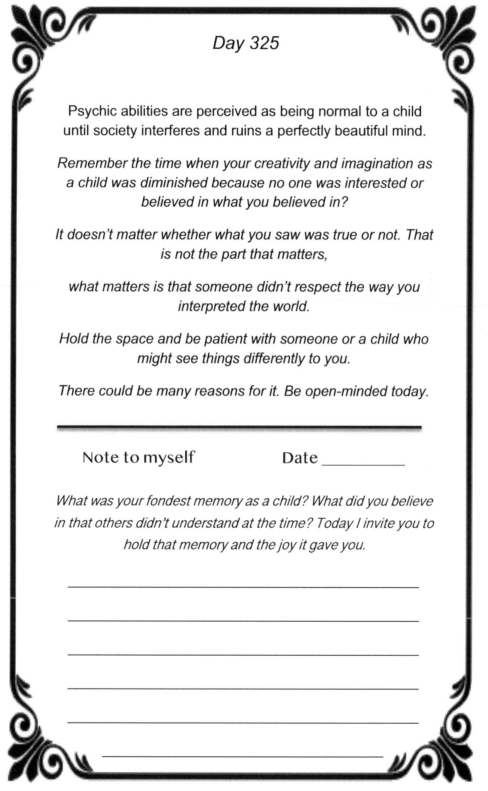

Day 325

Psychic abilities are perceived as being normal to a child until society interferes and ruins a perfectly beautiful mind.

Remember the time when your creativity and imagination as a child was diminished because no one was interested or believed in what you believed in?

It doesn't matter whether what you saw was true or not. That is not the part that matters,

what matters is that someone didn't respect the way you interpreted the world.

Hold the space and be patient with someone or a child who might see things differently to you.

There could be many reasons for it. Be open-minded today.

Note to myself   Date _____

What was your fondest memory as a child? What did you believe in that others didn't understand at the time? Today I invite you to hold that memory and the joy it gave you.

_____

_____

_____

_____

_____

_____

Day 326

If you are not determined and committed to seeing changes in your life and health, then no amount of education, dreams, or hopes will make it happen. The secret is self-belief and determination.

You have to set the wheel in motion if you want to see changes in your quality of life and if you don't, then your body will give you a reason to make those changes. Don't wait for the universe to provide you with a rude awakening. Look after yourself, if you are not doing well, if you are not feeling healthy, then how can you show up in a powerful and motivational way for others who look up to you?

Note to myself   Date _____

What is your definition of support? How can you allow yourself to be supported today?

_____

_____

_____

_____

_____

_____

_____

_____

Day 327

You cannot change people. If people don't want to change, then it's their choice. Let it be. People will change when they are ready and if they are not, often the time comes when the universe will bring forward circumstances to show them where change is needed.

Release yourself from this unnecessary obligation. You haven't failed anyone by not stepping in and taking charge of a situation when you can see that adjustments in their life / lifestyle are desperately needed. You can change yourself, though.

Note to myself   Date _____

Stay focused on your goals, needs and dreams. Make more time for yourself and embrace your talents. What steps can you take today to delve into your talents again?

_____

_____

_____

_____

_____

_____

_____

Day 328

Your goals and how they manifest is a result of the level of positivity, self-belief, and passion you invested in them.

Your life, goals and dreams are a reflection of your efforts.

If you feel that you have to fight for success, then that is exactly what you will experience.

If you are always waiting for others to find the solutions to your problems, then you will find yourself with conditional support and a path that will be controlled by someone, or you will simply fail.

Be in control of your state of mind, never give your power away to any judgment or criticism; there will always be people who want to see you fail.

The opposition will often be right on your heels.

Note to myself   Date _____

What is your definition of passion?

_____

_____

_____

_____

_____

_____

Day 329

When you lose your passion, the flame that kept your dreams alive gets put out.

Your goals lose their value, and that will ultimately be reflected in your self-esteem.

Remind yourself today, why you started that very thing that is associated with your passion.

Remember why you started your goals in the first place.

Remember the excitement, drive, and self-belief.

Often we only need to be reminded of that which ignited that flame within us that propelled us toward this goal.

It could also be that you need a change of plan and approach. New people in your life that can support your vision.

When you explore this, you will find the answer, and you will know what needs to be corrected.

The secret is never to give up.

Note to myself   Date _____

In relation to your most passionate goal, how far do you feel you have come? What can you do differently today if you find yourself challenged or stuck?

_____

_____

Day 330

Meditation is essential, it's not just a 'mystical' exercise, it gives you the ability to truly hear what it is that you need to know and do to reconnect with your true authentic identity and inner peace.

Your pursuit of happiness will no longer be an effort. It's vital that you have your own space and time to be creative

Note to myself   Date _____

What can you do differently today to make more time to do what you love?

_____

_____

_____

_____

_____

_____

_____

_____

_____

_____

_____

Day 331

Your thoughts, feelings and how you show up in life is determined by your life experiences.

This also includes predisposed ancestral life experiences and aspects of your parent's dominant genes that are affected and triggered by your environment and circumstances.

You are in control of your emotional wellbeing. That is good news. How you allow this to be expressed out in your life is up to you. You are not a victim of your past or inherited genes. You are a creator of new and creative mental solutions.

Note to myself   Date _____

Your mindset is the most powerful tool that you will have in this life. What kind of mindset will bring you closer to your deepest desire?

_____

_____

_____

_____

_____

_____

_____

Day 332

Wake up, be awesome, be graceful, own your brand, stand in your power, and show kindness and then repeat.

It doesn't matter what you kick start in life, whether it's a personal goal or a professional goal. You have to own what you do and take on in life. Be dedicated to what you want to achieve; it will not be accomplished with a doubtful approach. Make sure that what you want to do is in alignment with your heart. Ask yourself, "Do I want this?" If the answer is yes, then stand in your power, show kindness, and be loyal and disciplined to your goals.

Note to myself   Date _____

Write down your definition of success. What steps can you take or mindset can you adapt to today to embody this definition?

_____

_____

_____

_____

_____

_____

_____

_____

Day 333

Words have the power to create a lasting impact when it's expressed and delivered with love, kindness, and compassion.

Your positivity is channeled into the vibration of these words and can be felt by a broken heart.

Be mindful today of the words that you speak and the intention behind those words.

If you are trying to be kind, yet feel resentful, then the resentment will be channeled through your message that was intended to be helpful.

We are all intuitive, and we can all feel when someone is not sincere.

I invite you today to be mindful of what you say and how you say it. Show kindness today and allow your emotional state to be in alignment with your words.

Note to myself   Date _____

Speak kind words toward yourself.

Hold positive thoughts toward yourself.

Write down five things that you love about yourself.

_____

_____

_____

Day 334

Your thoughts dominate the quality of your life. Remember, those thoughts are there for a reason.

If they are negative, then it's essential that you resolve the reason that gave birth to the negative thoughts and feelings. It will lead you back to your true authentic self; you will rediscover your inner peace again.

Note to myself   Date _____

Write down your most dominant negative thought today. Give the thought an independent voice. What would it say? What is the hidden message behind this thought?

_____

_____

_____

_____

_____

_____

_____

_____

_____

_____

_____

Day 335

Only act on words and actions that resonate with your heart.

Sometimes your mind can betray you, it's affected by fear and thoughts that shape and filter out the positive circumstances and healthy relationships in your life. Your true authenticity lays within. Be still and listen.

Note to myself   Date _____

Being silent with ourselves can be frightening, as we feel what we don't want to feel or become aware of. I invite you today be silent for 10 minutes and instead of feeling anxious, find peace within the silence. After this exercise write down your biggest worries and then write the opposite flip side to these worries.

_____

_____

_____

_____

_____

_____

_____

_____

Day 336

Karma is part of the universal law - Karma is the universe's way of correcting intentions, vibrations, and actions that are out of alignment with its ability to function and evolve.

It is essential that we are mindful of how we contribute to life and other people's lives.

The intention is to bring out the best in others and allow ourselves to grow and be part of a community that is working toward a collective goal.

That goal can take so many forms.

What matters is that we work together in harmony, supporting one another and extend a helping hand to those who are in need.

Peace has never been achieved by force.

Note to myself   Date _____

In which aspect of your life do you feel lack of peace? If there are many areas, then write down the most dominant one. What steps can you take today to bring more peace into that aspect of your life?

_____

_____

_____

_____

Day 337

You have so much to look forward to in life. Often a negative state of mind is the result of past experiences that shaped the filters in your neural pathways which block wonderful possibilities that are right in front of you.

Letting go of what no longer serves you is not just about forgiving or moving on; it creates a brand new powerful life that will set you free!

Note to myself   Date _____

What will your life look like and feel like in 1 years' time if you don't make positive changes in your life?

_____

_____

_____

_____

_____

_____

_____

_____

_____

_____

Day 338

When you reach a point when you feel you have reached the end, then you know it's time to change. It's time to reclaim your sense of self, that is where your power quietly rests. You are designed to survive, be resourceful, and adapt. Let go of the people who never believed in you, invite in the people who will.

You might be faced with a time in your life when you feel you have reached the end. But it's only the beginning of something new and amazing.

Note to myself   Date _____

Write down your definition of self-motivation.

_____

_____

_____

_____

_____

_____

_____

_____

_____

_____

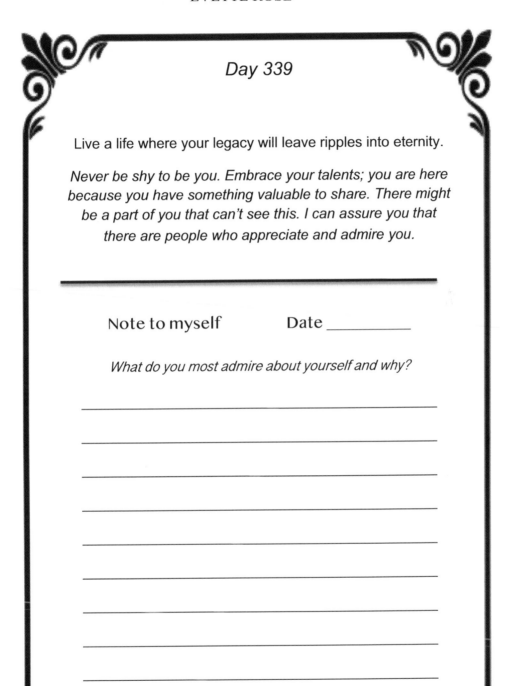

Day 339

Live a life where your legacy will leave ripples into eternity.

Never be shy to be you. Embrace your talents; you are here because you have something valuable to share. There might be a part of you that can't see this. I can assure you that there are people who appreciate and admire you.

Note to myself   Date _____

What do you most admire about yourself and why?

_____

_____

_____

_____

_____

_____

_____

_____

_____

_____

_____

Day 340

Nothing in life is ever lost neither; is it designed and started from scratch. Instead, it's either suppressed or it just transformed. Energy and matter never cease to exist. How you perceive it can lead you to believe that it no longer exists.

What you see is not always the truth. The perceived reality is also not still the absolute truth. We all have our way of interpreting what we see and feel. I invite you today to be open to new perspectives, observe, learn, and listen.

Note to myself   Date _____

Write down the last misunderstanding / miscommunication you had with someone. Then write down how you think they perceived the situation and how you perceived the situation. Observe the differences and why they were there in the first place.

_____

_____

_____

_____

_____

_____

_____

Day 341

The way to find what you truly are searching for in your life will only be revealed when you delve deep inside and give your heart and thoughts the time and attention they deserve.

Give them a voice and let them speak. No one can give you the answers that you are looking for, they can guide you, but ultimately, you are the only person who will know which path in life will set you free. A way that was patiently waiting to be discovered. You will only delay your progress in life when you keep searching for answers outside of yourself.

Note to myself   Date _____

Are you still waiting for permission to be powerful? Are you waiting for 'the right time' to step into your power? Do you have positive associations with being powerful? Let the answers to these questions wake you up. It's time to move forward, resistance has never shown you any positive results, why keep a pattern that no longer serves you.

_____

_____

_____

_____

_____

_____

_____

Day 342

Your mind is the most powerful tool that you will ever have, when you energize it with negative thoughts will respond and only allow you to see negativity.

When you energize it with positivity, you will see more positivity. When you energize it with opportunities, you will start to see wonderful opportunities that were never there before.

Today I invite you to choose wisely the state of mind you wish to be in, as it will determine how your day begins and ends. You can either set yourself up for failure or success.

Note to myself   Date _____

Make a conscious decision today about how you are going to show up.

_____

_____

_____

_____

_____

_____

_____

_____

Day 343

When you have no clear set of goals, structure, or direction in your life, you will have no passion!

You are the one that can set things in motion. People are only resources that can support you, but you have to be the driver and know where you are heading to! Your state of confusion will reflect in your internal and external world.

Note to myself   Date _____

In which aspect of your life do you need more clarity and planning? What can you do differently today to create more structure in your daily routine that will bring more structure?

_____

_____

_____

_____

_____

_____

_____

_____

_____

_____

Day 344

Loyalty is not just between friends and people in relationships. It's a relationship that you have with yourself.

Be loyal to your goals, your values, your needs, and most importantly, yourself.

Note to myself   Date _____

In which aspect of your life have you abandoned an important goal? What can you do today to reignite this goal once again?

_____

_____

_____

_____

_____

_____

_____

_____

_____

_____

_____

_____

_____

_____

Day 345

Everything is energy! Your thoughts start as emotion, and an emotion creates a reaction.

Understanding where the thought came from in the first place can turn a negative pattern and energetic cycle into a constructive and powerful pattern that will lead you to success and emotional freedom.

Your feelings and thoughts are powerful.

If you energize negative thoughts, then that is what you will see in your life. If you invest in positive thoughts, then that is exactly what you will see.

One reminder, though, you can't think yourself into a happier place and way of life. Find the source that caused the negative thought and feeling.

Take active steps to let go, heal, and move forward with the utmost curiosity of what the world can offer you.

Note to myself   Date _____

Doors will open when you are free from baggage that used to influence your state of mind and quality of life. What do you feel ready to let go of today? What small active steps can you start to take today to start the letting go process?

_____

_____

_____

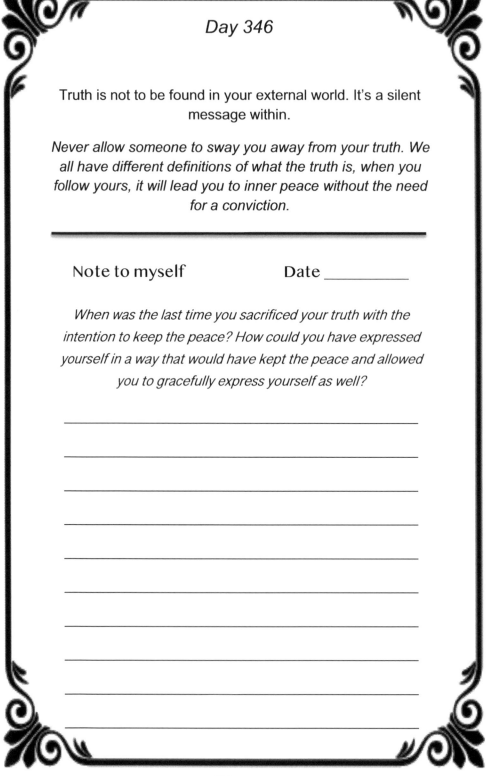

Day 346

Truth is not to be found in your external world. It's a silent message within.

Never allow someone to sway you away from your truth. We all have different definitions of what the truth is, when you follow yours, it will lead you to inner peace without the need for a conviction.

Note to myself   Date _____

When was the last time you sacrificed your truth with the intention to keep the peace? How could you have expressed yourself in a way that would have kept the peace and allowed you to gracefully express yourself as well?

_____

_____

_____

_____

_____

_____

_____

_____

_____

_____

Day 347

Be an observer today, be in silence and observe that which is around you. Observe the people in your life, friendships, and relationships.

Become aware of how you are contributing to these connections and how they are contributing to you.

See the good part of you that is within that connection and know that who you are and what you do is good enough.

We often underestimate how valuable we are. What we do is not just an effort; it's a service to the world

"Everyone has been made for some particular work, and the desire for that work has been put in every heart." ~ Rumi

---

Note to myself   Date _____

You are loved and appreciated in this life. Just because you can't see it, doesn't mean that these feelings are not alive in someone else's heart. Don't be dependent on confirmation and feedback, just know that how you show up and what you contribute is valuable to someone. Where in your life have you failed to recognize your importance and contribution to someone else's life or circumstances?

_____

_____

_____

_____

Day 348

No one can tell you something that you don't already know deep within. Just because you can't see or feel the answer, doesn't mean it's not already there. Sometimes you need to be reminded.

Allow yourself to be open to people and words of wisdom that can help reignite your inner voice. You are already set up for success, happiness, and abundance. It's just a matter of remembering.

Note to myself   Date _____

Who or what in your life caused you to underestimate yourself? What do you need to believe in yourself to know that you are so much more than what you thought you were?

_____

_____

_____

_____

_____

_____

_____

_____

Day 349

You are always right. If you think that you are going to fail, then you are right! If you believe that you are going to succeed, then you are right!

Believing in yourself is the most powerful inner resource that you can experience. When you are in this state of mind, no one can sway you from your path, your dreams, and goals.

Note to myself   Date _____

Do you believe in yourself? If you feel that this part of you has been suppressed then find the source that swayed you away from this powerful state of mind. I invite you today to hold the feeling of a wish fulfilled. Write down what it will look and feel like.

_____

_____

_____

_____

_____

_____

_____

_____

_____

Day 350

If you have a thought, yet your heart feels incoherent with that thought, then it's a recipe for inner turmoil. Find the conflict that is within, as your true authentic self is trying to communicate with you.

Take at least ten minutes today; go within. Explore the negative thought and feel into what your heart is feeling, then ask yourself which feeling or decision brings you the most peace?

Note to myself   Date _____

Focus on the answer that you receive and start making small changes to nurture this new thought or direction you need to take. Write down 5 things that you have successfully done and completed that you feel proud of. Then, write down the state of mind you had during those phases of your life. What can you do today to reconnect to that?

_____

_____

_____

_____

_____

_____

_____

_____

Day 351

You cannot search for peace. Peace will find you when you stop fighting for peace. You cannot experience peace when you are in a state of fighting for it; you are moving towards this goal backwards.

A lot can be achieved when you fight for it, but there is a time and a place for this approach.

Learn when to let go and when to move forward. Remember, if you are ever in doubt never make a decision, never make a promise you cannot fulfill.

Your inner peace is a state of mind that you can access when you meditate or be quiet within yourself by yourself. Who you are is peaceful, stop fighting for it, stop searching for it, and learn to become present with it.

Note to myself   Date _____

Use your discernment today to evaluate what is worth fighting for. What in your life have you been fighting for that is no longer of value to you?

_____

_____

_____

_____

_____

Day 352

The thoughts that you nurture is what you create in your life. The emotions that you hold in your heart is what you attract in life. What you envision for yourself you can become.

Become aware today of the thoughts and feelings that you nurture. Are they healthy for you? Are they going to help you create and attract everything you need to succeed in your professional and personal life?

Note to myself   Date _____

Your mission today, if you choose to accept it, is to become aware of what you are feeling and how the world is responding to you. Then, write down small steps and solutions to the challenges that you feel.

_____

_____

_____

_____

_____

_____

_____

_____

_____

Day 353

Eternal love is powered by unconditional acceptance. If what you desire is true love or friendship, then you have to nurture it.

Learn to listen and learn to be present. Love and friendship have no words or language; there is understanding and harmony even in the midst of a storm.

Be in sync with those you love. Learn to listen to one another; keep the communication channels open.

Be respectful of one another's values, goals, and needs. Most importantly of all, make sure that your goals, dreams, and values are in alignment.

It is a recipe for true love, acceptance, and friendship.

Note to myself   Date _____

Have you been a good listener lately? If you have been towards your loved ones, have you been a good listener towards yourself lately? If not, then why?

_____

_____

_____

_____

_____

_____

Day 354

There comes the point in your life when you suddenly realize that being yourself is not necessarily a virtue. It requires courage, self-belief, and fearlessness.

I invite you today to be yourself. Not the person that your parents' wanted you to be. Not the person that your boss, colleagues, or partner wants you to be. Not the person that your religion or family values wish you to be. Just be you. Scary thought, right?

Note to myself   Date _____

Who are you when all of the above is ripped away from who you thought you were? How will you show up in life? What decisions will you make and how will you make them? What would it feel like to live a life from your heart and not one that was dictated or imposed onto you? Who you are today will be the result of love, positive influence and guidance, but what about the influences that were not so positive? Become aware of your true identity. You just might be pleasantly surprised.

_____

_____

_____

_____

_____

_____

Day 355

Honor your needs, values, and desires. Be brave enough to speak up when your identity is suppressed and challenged. Be brave enough to walk away.

Sometimes we become so accustomed to a way life that we often fail to see how unhealthy our life has become. We fail to see how toxic some people are. We fail to respect our boundaries, self-worth, and values. We often sacrifice our identity for the sake of peace and acceptance.

Note to myself   Date _____

One word of advice, acceptance and peace should never come at a price, especially if you are the one paying it.

_____

_____

_____

_____

_____

_____

_____

_____

_____

_____

Day 356

You know that your true authentic self wants to express love. Pass it on and watch it being returned to you!

Love has so many different definitions, depending on your background and how it has been shown to you, that will either make or break your definition of love. Real love is not ownership, it's not manipulation and it's not jealousy.

Note to myself   Date _____

Write down today what your definition of love is. It should be the kind of love that is realistic and not the kind of love that you see in movies or read in romantic novels. Then, as you look at what you wrote, ask yourself "Am I ready to receive this right now?" The answer to this question will show where improvement is needed in order for you to allow even more love into your life.

_____

_____

_____

_____

_____

_____

_____

_____

Day 357

I choose to make conscious and clear decisions instead of excuses. I am motivated and will no longer be held back. I want a life where my dignity is intact; I will let go of manipulative people. I want to be free and will no longer be at any anyone's mercy. If you have a problem with that, then you are not meant to be part of my new path.

Love and respect yourself enough to move away from people and circumstances that cause you pain, hold you, or sabotage your growth.

Note to myself   Date _____

Sometimes we cannot just walk away from circumstances, however you can have boundaries, gentling loving yet firm boundaries. But first, you have to learn to love yourself enough to know that you are worthy and deserving of having these boundaries. What do you need to believe in yourself in order to know that you can express your boundaries?

_____

_____

_____

_____

_____

_____

_____

Day 358

The universe is our home; all beings are our tribe and oneness our religion.

The world is our only home; everyone around you is part of you and the collective consciousness. Love and compassion are our religion and faith.

Our ego and body is what separates us from a world, consciousness, and way of life. A life that we often dream of, yet it is right in front of us.

Note to myself   Date _____

How has your ego sabotaged your happiness and your ability to bond with people and loved ones in your life?

_____

_____

_____

_____

_____

_____

_____

_____

_____

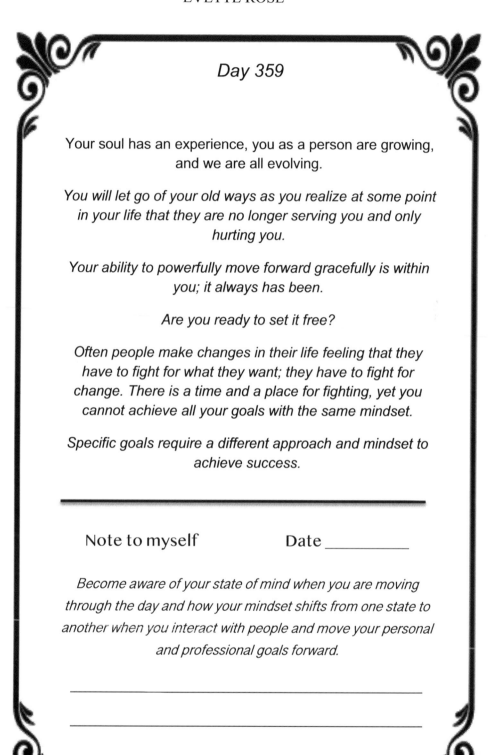

Day 359

Your soul has an experience, you as a person are growing, and we are all evolving.

You will let go of your old ways as you realize at some point in your life that they are no longer serving you and only hurting you.

Your ability to powerfully move forward gracefully is within you; it always has been.

Are you ready to set it free?

Often people make changes in their life feeling that they have to fight for what they want; they have to fight for change. There is a time and a place for fighting, yet you cannot achieve all your goals with the same mindset.

Specific goals require a different approach and mindset to achieve success.

Note to myself   Date _____

Become aware of your state of mind when you are moving through the day and how your mindset shifts from one state to another when you interact with people and move your personal and professional goals forward.

_____

_____

_____

Day 360

We all need interactions, connections, and conversations authentic people, true soul to soul conversations. Connect with people who speak to your soul and let the rest go and be part of your life experience and not part of your life.

Opening yourself up to others doesn't mean that you have to be vulnerable. It means that you should allow yourself to have the opportunity to connect with someone with discernment and an open mind.

Note to myself   Date _____

In which aspect of your life would you benefit more by being more open minded and flexible? What steps can you take today to start this?

_____

_____

_____

_____

_____

_____

_____

_____

_____

Day 361

I don't always know where I am heading. I can assure you though that I am going to make a big adventure out of it!

We don't always know where we are heading to in , and that is okay, it is okay to not always know. Stressing about it is only going to delay the right answer from coming to you with clarity. No one can keep a clear mind when they are stressed about something that hasn't even taken place yet.

Note to myself   Date _____

Be quiet, become aware of your fears, give them a voice and let them speak. When the energy of fear has been released, allow the true message to come forward.

_____

_____

_____

_____

_____

_____

_____

_____

_____

Day 362

When you criticize another, you are inevitably criticizing an unhealed part of yourself.

Often the answer to healing ourselves is right in front of us; it sometimes comes right out of our mouth.

When you find yourself being judgmental towards someone else today, see if there is a part of that person that you are suppressing within yourself.

Perhaps that person reminds you of a painful past or interaction with someone.

Find the source and heal it. As you judge, also be grateful, as these people are showing you the way toward a happier and healthier life.

Note to myself   Date _____

In which aspect of your life have you been judging yourself too much and why? What steps can you take today to be kinder toward yourself?

_____

_____

_____

_____

_____

_____

_____

Day 363

May all humans unite. May all women learn the sacredness of their femininity.

May all men learn the sacredness of their masculinity.

Allow yourself to be a graceful example for those who want to learn.

Love people while they make their mistakes.

Honor your elders as their wisdom and life experiences were passed down to you to learn from.

Embrace the voice of your soul. Take a minute today and become aware of everything that is around you; everything is alive in its own unique and special way.

Note to myself   Date _____

You are never alone, you are always part of everything that is around you. You as a human being are connected to a powerful collective consciousness and are always part of something greater. Just because you can't see it doesn't mean that it doesn't exist. Just because you can't hear or see certain frequencies, doesn't mean that they don't exist. You vibrate on your own level, yet that vibration is what's resonating in someone else. Honor the part of you that is in another and honor them in you. Be grateful, for you are never alone.

_____

_____

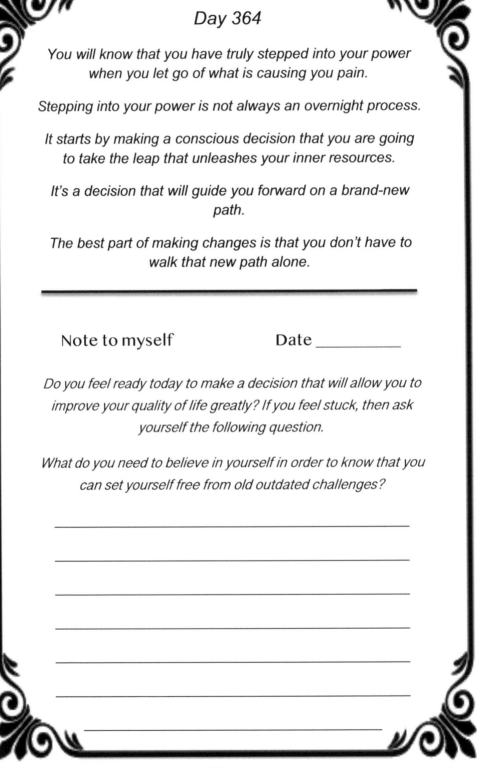

Day 364

You will know that you have truly stepped into your power when you let go of what is causing you pain.

Stepping into your power is not always an overnight process.

It starts by making a conscious decision that you are going to take the leap that unleashes your inner resources.

It's a decision that will guide you forward on a brand-new path.

The best part of making changes is that you don't have to walk that new path alone.

Note to myself   Date _____

Do you feel ready today to make a decision that will allow you to improve your quality of life greatly? If you feel stuck, then ask yourself the following question.

What do you need to believe in yourself in order to know that you can set yourself free from old outdated challenges?

_____

_____

_____

_____

_____

_____

_____

Day 365

As a river flows in harmony with the earth and the direction that it's being moved in2, so is our path to becoming the best version that we can be of ourselves. Resistance will cause a disruption in the flow.

Trusting your path and knowing that "this too shall pass" is easier said than done. Fighting your way forward will only rob you of love, happiness and being present with the people that you love.

Note to myself   Date _____

Explore today where you are mistrusting of your future. Instead of being frozen in fear, find a creative solution that can set the process of moving forward in motion. If you didn't feel stuck right now what would you be doing differently in your life?

_____

_____

_____

_____

_____

_____

_____

_____

Day 366

Love yourself and respect your needs and values. Just because others don't understand your path and your intentions, doesn't mean that you should give up.

It only means that the company you entertain has not taken the time to understand. Be OK with that. Move forward, fearlessly.

The right people who will support your cause will show up at the right time.

Just because you feel you need people who you can relate to right now only means that you are undermining your ability to achieve these goals on your own.

Note to myself   Date _____

Write down your definition of support. When you look at your definition, do you feel this is present in your life? If the answer is no, then what steps can you take today to bring in more healthy support?

_____

_____

_____

_____

_____

_____

_____

Day 367

Start by making one healthy choice today, whether it's dietary, emotional or professional.

Make a choice that will benefit you emotionally or physically. Put yourself first.

We all get caught up in our daily routine, looking after loved ones and other people's needs, that we end up neglecting our own needs.

Today your mission, if you choose to accept it, is to finally do that one thing that you have been holding off, no more delays! Or make that healthy dietary change that your body is begging you for. Today is about 'me, myself and I.'

Note to myself   Date _____

Write down three health changes that you can make in your life today.

_____

_____

_____

_____

_____

_____

_____

_____

_____

Evette Rose is an Author, Life Coach, Co-Founder of a personal development company and founder of Metaphysical Anatomy, Evette was born in South Africa and grew up in Namibia, West Africa. She moved to Australia for work. She is best known for her work in helping people to resolve trauma from their past and freeing them to live successful and fulfilling lives. Evette's work is drawn from her personal experience of moving from a difficult past into a well-balanced life and career. Evette's philosophy is that we, as a human race, are not destined to live our lives in pain due to past trauma or abuse. Humans often suppress their ability to complete or heal trauma naturally. In today's society, we often suppress our pain to keep up with life and avoid being left behind. Fortunately, through gentle therapy, this natural internal healing instinct can be restored. Writing her books have helped Evette reach out to other people who need of love, support, and someone to relate to. She shares her experiences with the world in hopes that it will help people heal and provide encouragement and reassurance when they need it most. Evette now travels the world teaching personal development seminars. She has been to more than 43 countries and worked with thousands of people!

Would you like to learn and see more? Then visit my website:
www.metaphysicalanatomy.com

Printed in Great
Britain
by Amazon